Attributes of Splendour

Reflections on the nature, being, and glory of God

Dr. Ken Chant

Attributes of Splendour

Reflections on the nature, being, and glory of God

By *Ken Chant*

Copyright 2013 © Ken Chant

ISBN 978-1-61529-096-3

Vision Publishing
1672 Main Street E 109
Ramona, CA 92065
1 800-9-VISION
www.booksbyvision.com

All rights reserved worldwide. No part of this book may be reproduced in any manner without the written permission of the author except in brief quotations embodied in critical articles or reviews.

A NOTE ON GENDER

It is unfortunate that the English language does not contain an adequate generic pronoun (especially in the singular number) that includes without bias both male and female. So "he, him, his, man, mankind," with their plurals, must do the work for both sexes. Accordingly, wherever it is appropriate to do so in the following pages, please include the feminine gender in the masculine, and vice versa.

FOOTNOTES

A work once fully referenced will thereafter be noted either by "ibid" (the same) or "op. cit." (the work previously cited).

Contents

One: Apology 5
Two: Uncertainty 15
Three: Glory 19
Four: Words 29
Five: Reasons 35
Six: Trees 41
Seven: Wagering 51
Eight: Blame 61
Nine: Unity 77
Ten: Harmony 91
Eleven: Enthroned 97
Twelve: Love 105
Thirteen: Holiness 113
Fourteen: Powerful 121
Fifteen: Everywhere 131
Sixteen: Prescience 139
Seventeen: Foreknowledge 147
Eighteen: Openness 161
Nineteen: Prophecy 173
Twenty: Providence 181
Twenty-one: Immutable 193
Twenty-two: Timeless 201
Addenda 215

ABBREVIATIONS

Abbreviations commonly used for the books of the Bible are

Genesis	Ge	Habakkuk	Hb
Exodus	Ex	Zephaniah	Zp
Leviticus	Le	Haggai	Hg
Numbers	Nu	Zechariah	Zc
Deuteronomy	De	Malachi	Mal
Joshua	Js		
Judges	Jg		
Ruth	Ru	Matthew	Mt
1 Samuel	1 Sa	Mark	Mk
2 Samuel	2 Sa	Luke	Lu
1 Kings	1 Kg	John	Jn
2 Kings	2 Kg	Acts	Ac
1 Chronicles	1 Ch	Romans	Ro
2 Chronicles	2 Ch	1 Corinthians	1 Co
Ezra	Ezr	2 Corinthians	2 Co
Nehemiah	Ne	Galatians	Ga
Esther	Es	Ephesians	Ep
Job	Jb	Philippians	Ph
Psalm	Ps	Colossians	Cl
Proverbs	Pr	1 Thessalonians	1 Th
Ecclesiastes	Ec	2 Thessalonians	2 Th
Song of Songs	Ca *	1 Timothy	1 Ti
Isaiah	Is	2 Timothy	2 Ti
Jeremiah	Je	Titus	Tit
Lamentations	La	Philemon	Phm
Ezekiel	Ez	Hebrews	He
Daniel	Da	James	Ja
Hosea	Ho	1 Peter	1 Pe
Joel	Jl	2 Peter	2 Pe
Amos	Am	1 John	1 Jn
Obadiah	Ob	2 John	2 Jn
Jonah	Jo	3 John	3 Jn
Micah	Mi	Jude	Ju
Nahum	Na	Revelation	Re

Ca is an abbreviation of *Canticles,* a derivative of the Latin name of the *Song of Solomon,* which is sometimes also called the *Song of Songs.*

Note: scripture translations are my own unless otherwise noted.

ONE

APOLOGY

Montaigne once wrote – [1]

> Here are the excretions of an ageing mind, sometimes thick, sometimes thin, and always indigested. I wonder if I shall ever have done with penning the continual agitation and mutation of my thoughts, as they come into my head, seeing that Diomedes wrote six thousand books upon the sole subject of grammar?
>
> What, then, ought one's prating to produce, since the prattling of an infant, when mankind first began to speak, has now stuffed the world with such a horrible load of volumes? So many words about words only! ...
>
> But there should be some restraint of law against foolish and impertinent scribblers, as well as against vagabonds and idle persons; which if there were, both I and a hundred others would be banished from the reach of our people. I do not speak this in jest – scribbling seems to be a symptom of a disordered and licentious age. When did we write so much as since our civil wars; when the Romans so

---

(1) Essays of Michel de Montaigne (1533-1592), translated (1877) by Charles Cotton, edited by William Carew Hazlitt, with a few clarifications added by myself; Bk III, Ch. 9.

much, as when they were upon the point of ruin? ...

However, 'tis my comfort, that I shall be one of the last who shall be called in question; and whilst the greater offenders are being brought to account, I shall have leisure to amend: for it would, methinks, be against reason to punish little inconveniences, whilst we are infested with the greater. As the physician Philotimus said to one who presented him his finger to dress, and who he perceived, both by his complexion and his breath, had an ulcer in his lungs: "Friend, it is not now time to play with your nails."

I cannot help but share a little of Montaigne's discomfort. Among the countless books already in existence on the attributes of God, why add another? Will it be any better than they? Probably not? Will it say anything truly new? Very doubtful! So why? Well, I do have some things that I want to say, and I will perhaps say at least some of them differently, and I may manage to tread upon a new path here and there. I might even deserve the encomium that Alexander Pope composed in 1715 to "an ingenious friend" –

> Tho' many a Wit from time to time has rose
> *T'inform* the World of what it *better knows*,
> Yet 'tis a Praise that few their own can call,
> To tell men things they never *knew at all*. [2]

Or if some insist that I have not said anything new, at least I may wish that they will enjoy the way I have said it! I hope

---

(2) To My Ingenious Friend, lines 1-4.

that when you reach the end of this book, your judgment may echo Addison's comment on writing –

> Wit and fine Writing doth not consist so much in advancing Things that are new, as in giving Things that are known an agreeable Turn. It is impossible for us, who live in the latter Ages of the World, to make Observations in Criticism, Morality, or in any Art or Science, which have not been touched upon by others. We have little else left us, but to represent the common Sense of Mankind in more strong, more beautiful, or more uncommon Lights. If a Reader examines *Horace's Art of Poetry,* he will find but very few Precepts in it, which he may not meet with in *Aristotle,* and which were not commonly known by all the Poets of the *Augustan* Age. His Way of expressing and applying them, not his Invention of them, is what we are chiefly to admire. (3)

So if you cannot praise me for saying something new, I hope at least that you will find I have given familiar things an "agreeable turn", and that what I might lack in "invention" has been compensated by some facility in "expressing and applying" the truth of scripture.

Another reason for this book is that my two volumes on Christ (4) need their complement in a book about the Father and about the entire Godhead.

---

(3)   Joseph Addison in The Spectator, # 253, December 20th, 1711.
(4)   Emmanuel *Volumes One & Two.* See also The Cross and the Crown.

But my chief reason for burdening the planet with this seemingly redundant volume lies in the subject itself. The Lord God is my Lord, and to me he is so fascinating that I cannot resist the yearning to explore every facet of his splendour, hoping that others will thereby be able to share my pleasure. I hope, too, that the Father himself will be pleased with what I write and that, even if only in a small way, his honour will be enlarged.

Montaigne trusted that his scribblings would not cause him to be condemned, or at least, if he were found guilty, that his fault would be accounted small and his punishment slight. Again I echo his sentiment, although perhaps with less assurance. The theme of these pages rises much higher than any addressed by the Frenchman, and therefore may cause more furious controversy. I cannot hope that all will agree with all that they read here. In the main I am orthodox in my views, but if I dislike the common opinion on a matter I do not hesitate to voice dissent. Some of what follows will express ideas that differ from, or at least modify, what some scholars reckon orthodox. I ask only that you read with an open mind, and if you choose to disagree with me on an occasional point, then do so with my blessing. You are but exercising the sweet liberty that God has given us all – to act in harmony with conscience, and to choose honestly for ourselves what is right and what is wrong. [5] In the meantime, I hope that I may claim for myself the words of Isaiah –

> *The Lord God has given me the tongue of a teacher, so that by my words I may encourage and strengthen the weary. Every morning as I*

---

(5)   1 John 2:27; 1 Thessalonians 5:21; 1 John 4:1; Philippians 1:10.

awaken he makes me eager to learn what his next teaching will be. (50:4)

VARIOUS CLASSIFICATIONS

Standard approaches to a study of *The Attributes of God* tend to follow a form similar to the examples that follow.

Example One –

- *Metaphysically* – God is Self-existent, Eternal, and Unchanging.
- *Intellectually* – God is Omniscient, Faithful, and Wise.
- *Ethically* – God is Holy, Righteous, and Loving.
- *Emotionally* – God Detests Evil, is Longsuffering, and Compassionate.
- *Existentially* – God is Free, Authentic, and Omnipotent.
- *Relationally* – God is Transcendent in Being, but Immanent Universally. (6) That is, he is active in providence, and in the redemption of his people. (7)

Example Two –

- God's Inner Nature (Unrelated Attributes)
- God is a Spirit

---

(6) Note: "imm<u>a</u>nent" is not the same as "imm<u>i</u>nent". The latter means that "something is going to happen soon". The former, when applied to God, means the nearness of God to his creation, and in particular to his people.

(7) From the Evangelical Dictionary of Theology; ed. Walter A. Elwell; article *God, Attributes of*, by G. R. Lewis; Baker Book House, Grand Rapids, 1984; pg. 451-459.

- God is Infinite
- God is One
- God in Relation to the Universe (Active Attributes)
- God is Omnipotent
- God is Omnipresent
- God is Omniscient
- God is Wise
- God is Sovereign
- God in Relation to Moral Creatures (Moral Attributes)
- God is Holy
- God is Righteous
- God is Faithful
- God is Merciful
- God is Good [8]

Example Three –

- The Incommunicable Attributes
- The Self-Existence of God
- The Immutablity of God
- The Infinity of God
- The Unity of God
- The Communicable Attributes
- The Spirituality of God
- Intellectual Attributes

---

(8) From <u>Knowing the Doctrines of the Bible</u>, by Myer Pearlman; Gospel Publishing House, Springfield; 1937; pg. 57-68.

- Moral Attributes
- Attributes of Sovereignty [9]

Various other classifications have been conceived over the centuries, but none of them has gained universal recognition. They all suffer from a measure of falsehood; they all fail to encompass the infinite glory of God.

In particular, those that try to divide God into bits that he can share with humans and bits that he cannot share, seem to be truly dubious. From one point of view, everything that appertains to the deity has been in some slight measure placed in us who are made in his image. From another point of view, "none of the divine perfections are communicable in the infinite perfection in which they exist in God." [10]

A SERIES OF MEDITATIONS

So then, how shall we approach the subject? My first intention was in fact to adopt a formal outline, similar to the three examples above, with some variations of my own. But the more I worked on it, the less I liked it. Somehow, I felt as if I were violating the splendour of the Lord, that I was trying to imprison the Infinite in small boxes of my own making.

I finally decided to abandon theological formality, and to present my thoughts, not in the usual style, but rather as a series of reflections, or meditations. I hope this will help the book to seem like a loving discussion with the Father rather than a chilly exercise in logical dogma.

---

(9) From <u>Systematic Theology</u>, by Louis Berkhof; Banner of Truth Trust, Edinburgh; 1976; pg. 57-81.

(10) Ibid. pg. 56. Berkhof, however, as the outline above shows, does finally choose to divide the attributes of God into those that are incommunicable to humans, and those that are communicable.

Consequently, this volume may lack some coherence, and certainly lacks completeness. A full study of the divine attributes would occupy several hundred more pages than you will find here. If you really wish to study the theme exhaustively then turn to the internet. You will easily find thousands of pages dealing with every aspect of the doctrine of God!

Montaigne says that the eminent Greek physician Philotimus (4th century BC) scolded a man who was worried about a sore finger when he had an ulcerated lung. Jesus rebuked the Pharisees for the same folly – straining out gnats while they swallowed camels [11] – and theologians, too, have often been guilty of majoring on minors and minoring on majors. Nowhere is that more true than here. Church leaders have excommunicated each other and banished entire groups of churches into outer darkness simply because of some difference of opinion about this or that aspect of God's being, nature, and attributes. Yet their dogma has sometimes rested more upon human reason than upon biblical revelation – or else they frequently place more weight on a verse than it can sensibly carry – or they build a doctrine by collecting only certain passages while relegating others to the dustbin. The result is dogma that says more about its creators than it does about God!

Perhaps I am guilty of the same folly. I hope not. Yet while I know that some extension of scripture is unavoidable, I have tried to do as little of it as possible. You will have to judge for yourself whether my aspiration has been more noble than my achievement.

---

(11) Matthew 23:24. The anecdote about Philotimus is mentioned in the quote from Montaigne that heads this meditation. The numerous works of Philotimus, of which only a few fragments are still extant, are often quoted by ancient writers.

But this is certainly true – *the only infallible thing in this world is the Word of God itself*, not human interpretations of that Word. So beware when anyone (myself included) seems to be pressing beyond what the Bible actually says. Perhaps they speak truly; perhaps they don't!

At least I will say this, that when the Bible declines to spell out a matter clearly, and I do find myself obliged to fill in at least some of the gaps, I know what I am doing. Consequently, I refuse to get angry when someone chooses to use a different filler. They have as much right – if they act in godly sincerity – to their opinion as I have to mine.

On the doctrine of God, the Bible shows admirable restraint, and leaves many questions unanswered. We too should be content with a little darkness and resist the urge to wrap the Lord God into our faulty definitions and shackle him with our far from infallible creeds.

So my purpose here is not to explain God, for that is impossible. My desire is simply to set down some thoughts and ideas that I hope will enrich your life and will be taken as the witness of a loving and worshipful believer to the glory of the Lord.

TWO

UNCERTAINTY

> Now, my tongue, the mystery telling
> of the glorious Body sing,
> and the Blood, all price excelling,
> which the gentiles' Lord and King,
> in a Virgin's womb once dwelling,
> shed for this world's ransoming. (12)

Can we truly know *anything*? The lines above echo the Bible in describing even the gospel as a *"mystery"* that lies beyond final human comprehension. But the same is true of many other things –

> "All that is certain is that nothing is certain."
> (Sextus Empiricus)

Socrates was reported as saying that he knew nothing except that he knew nothing.

Arcesilas, a philosopher of the *New Academy*, went even further than Socrates and declared that we could not even be certain that nothing was certain.

William of Ockham (c. 1300-49) argued that it was impossible to prove by human reason that God is infinite or omniscient or even that there is one God rather than many.

Nicholas of Cusa, following St Paul, presented Christianity as a form of folly which is superior to wisdom.

---

(12) St Thomas Aquinas (13th century), tr. by Edward Caswall (1848); 1st. stanza.

So much for certainty! Indeed, most thoughtful people today acknowledge that all our knowledge in the end comprises nothing more than definitions of things, to make them comprehensible, or useful, or both, to us humans. Whether or not those definitions have any true connection with reality is another matter. A different set of intelligent beings, dwelling on some distant planet, might arrive at a vastly different set of equations, formulae, explanations, and the like. Rather like a group of chefs confronted with a variety of ingredients – using the same stuff, they can concoct widely different meals, or devise an amazing variety of recipes. The recipes are useful, but they hardly represent ultimate truth. So with all our formulations, whether scientific or theological. They have their place, and we could not function without them. But the vast universe is ignorant of them, and content to be so, and will go on its way without taking any of them into consideration!

With a hand of caution lifted, then, let us begin an exploration of the nature and being of our glorious God, never forgetting that nothing we say can be wholly true. Every creed that was ever devised trembles on the edge of heresy. The Spirit of God is like the wind that comes and goes as it pleases (Jn 3:8), and is averse to being pinned down. Indeed, who *can* confine the wind, or compel it to go here or there, to blow strong or weak? So there is an elusiveness about Christian doctrine that compels us to re-define it over and over again, yet never arriving at an infallible statement.

WHY SO MUCH CONFUSION?

One of the most startling assertions ever made by Paul concerns the decree of God that *human wisdom, by itself, will never succeed in discovering him*. Indeed, the Lord says that if, by thought alone, great thinkers begin to find him then he will confound their wisdom and turn it into nonsense (1 Co 1:19-20). The confusion that exists among secular thinkers and philosophers is therefore explained. God has resolved that he will be known only through the preaching of the gospel (vs. 18, 21-25). So no matter how hard they toil, nor how brilliant their thoughts, philosophers, using only philosophy, will never find God.

Yet among those who do believe, there remains room for wisdom of the highest sort, and also for the most profound humility – that is, recognition that truly we know nothing; or even if we may claim to know a little, that we know it like people who must look through a piece of smoky glass (1 Co 13:12). Many people, sage and fool alike, have been obliged to confess, "The older I get, the less I know!"

You may complain, "But surely there are *some* certainties?"

Indeed there are, especially those things that God has revealed concerning himself in scripture and through Christ. Those gospel realities truly are firm foundations upon which we may plant our feet, and believe, and know that we are safe for ever in the arms of God.

Yet still, while we know, we don't know, and many mysteries remain. So we face the paradox – especially when we try to encompass within the boundaries of finite words an Almighty and Infinite God – that every answer raises more questions, and some questions have no answers at all. Every word that follows in these pages is written with a sense of that limitation. There will be truth in what I write, but it cannot be wholly true, because the Lord God is simply too measureless to be measured, and too boundless to be confined.

But sufficient can be known to establish faith more strongly and to call up higher worship, which I pray will in the end be your experience.

THREE

GLORY

> O God, thou bottomless abyss!
> Thee to perfection who can know?
> O height immense! What words suffice
> Thy countless attributes to show?
> Unchangeable, all-perfect Lord,
> Essential life's unbounded sea;
> What lives and moves, lives by thy word;
> It lives, and moves, and is from thee. (13)

In the systematic theologies of the western churches, it has been common to divide the study of God into three sections – the _nature_ of the Godhead; the divine _attributes_; and God's _relation_ to the created universe.

These meditations follow a different pattern –

- I will not be examining the *natural proofs* of God's existence that are provided by his _works_, for they are part of my book *Strong Reasons*.
- Nor will I be examining the arguments for Trinitarian belief, for they are part of my book *Emmanuel – Parts One & Two*.
- Nor will I be examining the *Names of God*, for they are part of my books *Healing in the Whole Bible*, and *Throne Rights*. (14)

---

(13)   E. Lange; tr. by John Wesley; st. 1 & 5.

All that I plan to do here is to examine God's divine *attributes*, that is, those elements of his nature and being that reveal his character, his identity, his manner of working.

To know God is the greatest treasure – to live and die without knowing God is the greatest tragedy. But this knowledge of God is sacred, to be approached with care, recognising that every definition expressed in human categories must remain inadequate. [15]

There are two surprises that overtake anyone who seeks to know God –

- God is the most **knowable** being (Je 31:34; 24:7)
- God is the most **unknowable** being (1 Ti 6:15-16).

So perhaps the best way to arrive at a deeper understanding of God is through a study of his attributes, for they are the means by which he has revealed himself to men and women. These attributes do not reveal the entire truth about God, but only what he permits us to know. Nonetheless they do give access to a richer understanding of who God is and what things he is willing to do, both for his people and for humanity in general.

Theologians have used various approaches to explore the divine attributes, and there has been much debate about what constitutes an *attribute* as distinct from an *activity*. Most people would probably assume that God's activities do reveal his attributes. And indeed, apart from what is

---

(14) However, you will find some comment in these pages on all three of those items, albeit from a different perspective to the one followed in the three books mentioned.

(15) For an explanation of why this is so see *Addendum Number One* below.

specifically declared in scripture, we have no better way to discover who God *is* than by observing what he *does*.

Some have presented the attributes of God under these categories –

- **_unrelated attributes_** (God as he is and was in himself before the world began); and
- **_related attributes_** (God in relation to the physical world and to the moral world).

Others have preferred to use the categories, **_general attributes_**; and **_specific attributes_**.

I will simply deal with them as they come to mind, without any particular pattern or categorising. The list will not be complete (not that *any* listing could ever embrace *all* that God is), but I hope that enough will be presented to show the supernal glory of the Lord.

So then, what do we mean when we say *"God"*? The Church has commonly held that certain things must be affirmed about the God of the Bible and of our faith –

A SELF-EXISTENT GOD

All else that exists [16] is contingent upon the will and the work of God. He alone exists **necessarily**, has always existed, and can never cease to exist, being himself the sole cause of his own existence, for he has *"life in himself"* (Jn 5:26). Thus the child's question, "Who made God?" is a logical absurdity. [17] It is akin to asking, "Who made the one who is not made?" If one accepts the existence of God, as I

---

(16) Including the devil, demons, and the entire kingdom of darkness.
(17) For another logical absurdity, see below under "Omnipotence".

most certainly do, then one accepts also that he has always been, and is, and always will be, indestructible and almighty.

Very young children have no difficulty comprehending this, for they have no sense of their own beginning nor of their ending. Only as the years advance do they begin to understand the principle of cause and effect, and start to look for a cause of God. But he is the sole Uncaused being in the entire universe. His existence depends upon nothing but himself. Whatever else exists is his creation and is utterly contingent upon his will for its continuance.

What happens if the existence of an Uncaused God is denied? We are left with an absurdity –

> It has been argued by some that everything in the universe can be explained in terms of something else, and that in terms of something else again, and so on, in an infinite chain . . . However, it is quite wrong to suppose that an infinite chain of explanation is satisfactory on the basis that every member of that chain is explained by the next member. One is still left with the mystery of why that *particular* chain is the one that exists, or why any chain exists at all.
>
> Leibnitz made this point eloquently by inviting us to consider an infinite series of books, each one copied from a previous one. To say that the content of the book is thereby explained is absurd. We are still justified in asking who the author was. [18]

---

(18)   Paul Davies, <u>The Mind of God</u>, Simon & Schuster, London, 1992; pg. 15.

In any case, it is surely more difficult to believe in a mindless yet self-caused universe than in an all-wise self-caused God. *Something* has to be free of all contingency, the ultimate source and cause of everything else. That *something* we say is actually *Someone*, the glorious being whom we call God –

> Immortal, invisible, God only wise,
> In light inaccessible hid from our eyes,
> Most blessèd, most glorious, the Ancient of Days,
> Almighty, victorious, Thy great Name we praise.
> To all, life Thou givest, to both great and small;
> In all life Thou livest, the true life of all;
> We blossom and flourish as leaves on the tree,
> And wither and perish—but naught changeth Thee. (19)

A SELF-SUFFICIENT GOD

There is nothing God needs from outside himself, for he is already completely furnished with all that is necessary for undying and limitless joy; thus, except by his own choice, nothing can either enrich or impoverish him. Hence his name is *Yahweh* – he who exists eternally and sufficiently of himself.

We may ask then, "If God is completely self-sufficient, why did he create the universe? What need can he have for it? What can it add to his joy?"

- ***answer***: he created us for the happiness of giving happiness.

But then, does that not make God more happy than he was before?

---

(19)   Walter C. Smith (1876), Hymn, stanzas one & three.

- ***answer***: there is a point at which we confront inexplicable mystery in God (1 Ti 6:16); we can then do only two things –

ADMIT THE LIMITS OF OUR MINDS *(1 Co 13:9-12)*

> Flower in the crannied wall,
> I pluck you out of the crannies,
> I hold you here, root and all, in my hand,
> Little flower – but *if* I could understand
> What you are, root and all, and all in all,
> I should know what God and man is. [20]

Well of course neither poet, philosopher, physicist, nor priest can tell "all, and all in all" about even the most humble flower – or anything else. We can describe its attributes, even down to a sub-atomic level, but *why* it is so, or why it even is at all, defies the loftiest wisdom of man. If we cannot truly define a daisy, it is laughable to suppose that we can fully define the infinite God.

ADMIT THE LIMITS OF OUR WORDS

> Call it what you will, we call it a "Person". I suppose the expression is not entirely satisfactory; it is rather just a stammering about the matter (just as we stammer when we use the word "Trinity"). But what are we to do? We are unable to produce anything better. So then, the Father is not the Son, and yet the Son is begotten from eternity of the Father, and the Holy Ghost proceeds from God the Father and

---

(20) Alfred, Lord Tennyson, Flower in the Crannied Wall.

> from God the Son. There are, then, three Persons, and yet there is only one God. [21]

The fact is, whatever terms we use – god, person, trinity, godhead, substance, essence, and so on – are in the end inadequate and shadowed by heresy. But there are no other words available to us, and so we must do the best we can with them, and not press any of them so far that they actually do tumble into error. We speak about the "threeness" of God, or the "trinity", yet those words are perilous in their tendency to end up with three gods and not one. But then if we stress the "oneness" of God, we are in danger of denying the individuality of the Father, the Son, and the Spirit. In fact, no matter how careful we are, every sentence is infected with some poison of heresy. We can hope only that the Lord will overlook and forgive our stammerings as he sees in us a sincere desire to know him and love him better.

So, I must talk about one and only one Almighty God, yet I must also allow that in this one God there co-exist three Persons, for to do otherwise is to deny scripture. I worship only one Lord, God, Creator, yet within that Godhead I share a warm relationship with each of the Persons. Three-in-One, One-in-Three; Trinity in Unity, Unity in Trinity. One can spin words for ever and still arrive no closer to this God who dwells "in light inaccessible, hid from our eyes"!

Which leads well into the next thought –

---

(21) <u>What Luther Says</u>, compiled by Edward M. Plass; Concordia Pub. House, Saint Louis, Mo., 1959; Vol. Two, pg. 541. In this quote Martin Luther is speaking about a related but different subject, "How to define the Trinity," and in particular, the difficulty of finding "entirely satisfactory" names for each of the members of the Trinity. The problem, however, is much the same when it comes to defining anything about God. No words are adequate, and every definition eventually finds itself in conflict with another.

A TRIUNE GOD

The Larger Westminster Catechism of 1647 presents a nice statement of the doctrine of the Trinity –

Question 8: Are there more Gods than one?
Answer: There is but one only, the living and true God.

Question 9: How many persons are there in the Godhead?
Answer: There be three persons in the Godhead, the Father, the Son, and the Holy Ghost; and these three are one true, eternal God, the same in substance, equal in power and glory; although distinguished by their personal properties.

Question 10: What are the personal properties of the three persons in the Godhead?
Answer: It is proper to the Father to beget the Son, and to the Son to be begotten of the Father, and to the Holy Ghost to proceed from the Father and the Son from all eternity.

Question 11: How does it appear that the Son and the Holy Ghost are God equal with the Father?
Answer: The Scriptures manifest that the Son and the Holy Ghost are God equal with the Father, ascribing unto them such names, attributes, works, and worship, as are proper to God only.

The doctrine of the Trinity is one of the most difficult parts of Christian belief, and probably one of the chief things that offend unbelievers. [22] Yet it is demanded by the biblical data, which ascribe divine attributes to three Persons – the Father, the Son, and the Holy Spirit. Each of those beings is portrayed in scripture as possessing certain attributes that

---

(22)   For further comment on the Trinity, see meditations *Nine* and *Ten* below.

only the Supreme Being can hold. A person who possesses the *attributes* of God, especially those attributes that belong to deity alone, must *be* God.

Thus, while the Bible insists that there is only *one* God (De 6:4), it also shows that within that one Divine Being there are three Persons – the *Father*, the *Son*, and the *Holy Spirit*. In scripture these three are shown to be equal in glory and power, and they dwell together in absolute and eternal love. Though they each hold a different office, and may be thought of as acting separately at various times, yet whatever is done by one is done by all, for within the Godhead there is not the slightest division of purpose, nor do any of the Persons act without the others. [23]

Hence it is unthinkable that the Son would act against the will of the Father, or that the Holy Spirit would defy the purpose of the Son. This simple fact provides us with a good rule by which to measure whether or not something is true or correct. If you are inclined to accept some prompting as coming from the Holy Spirit, or if you see a presumed vision of Jesus, but you are being told to act against the will of God as revealed in scripture, then you know that you are being misled. All that we know of the Godhead arises from scripture, and neither Father, Son, nor Spirit will ever act, or prompt anyone else to act, in contradiction of scripture.

---

(23) See my book <u>Emmanuel</u>–*Parts One & Two* for a full exploration of the deity and the humanity of Christ, who is both Son of God and Son of Man.

FOUR

WORDS

> In my heart I find ascending
> Holy awe, with rapture blending,
> As this mystery I ponder,
> Filling all my soul with wonder,
> Bearing witness at this hour
> Of the greatness of God's power;
> Far beyond all human telling
> Is the power within him dwelling.
> Human reason, though it ponder,
> Cannot fathom this great wonder
> That Christ's body e'er remaineth
> Though it countless souls sustaineth
> And that he his blood is giving
> With the wine we are receiving.
> These great mysteries unsounded
> Are by God alone expounded. [24]

It has often been said that any attempt to define either God or even the attributes of God, must reduce the deity to a set of human categories, trying to limit him to a compilation of headings and sub-headings. All words, it is said, confine the Lord within the limits of the human mind, as if we could put the Eternal into a box, neatly labelled, and tied with a pretty ribbon. So it is claimed that words can tell us nothing about reality, for they are in the end (as Montaigne complained [25])

---

[24] Johann Franck (1649); tr. by Catherine Winkworth (1858); stanzas 5 & 6.

[25] See again the quote that heads my first meditation.

only "words about words". We invent a word to describe something, and thereafter our understanding of that object is limited by the meaning we give to the word associated with it. Job felt this frustration of quarrels about words –

> *How forceful are the words of an upright man! But as for your arguments, what do they prove? Do you mean to contend with me over the meaning of words? Will you treat my desperate speech as if it were nothing but thin air? (6:25-26)*

UNCERTAIN WORDS

Unhappily, we face the problem that the meaning of each word is never quite the same for each user, nor does it have just the same sense as the word chosen in a different culture or language to describe the same object, say, a tree or an animal, or, for that matter, God. In each place, and for each person, each word carries along with it a different burden of memories, images, colouring, associations, experiences, and emotions.

Further, human thought is limited by language – I can think only within the limits of the words I know, which places a severe restraint upon knowledge. And some things I will never know, because the language I use has no way to express them, although in another tongue they may be easy to say. Indeed, all languages enable their speakers to say some things that cannot be said, or not in the same way, in any other tongue.

WASTED WORDS?

For these reasons, some scholars have rather madly argued that language is entirely subjective, has no objective meaning at all, and that we can say nothing finally or absolutely about anything! Words, they say, are merely symbols, human inventions whose meaning rests wholly upon social convention. There is no more connection between a word and the thing it represents than a road sign has with the town it points to. And least of all, some argue, can we say anything meaningful about *God*. At best our words about God are nothing more than expansions of other words about God. They cannot escape their confines and actually meet God.

Now it is true that language is a tool used by us humans, and that it has only limited connection with reality. And it is true that we must distinguish between our words *about* God and the Almighty *himself*. But that cannot mean that our words have no value. For example, suppose I am describing a hurricane. Nothing I say or think can have any effect upon the real power of a shrieking wind – my words, indeed, can never be more than an indistinct echo of the real thing.

Nonetheless, those words do have meaning; they do convey at least some idea of the nature of a gale, its force, its causes, and its impact upon an observer.

Or think about the wonder of human love. Despite millions of words, does anyone even yet understand its sweet mysteries (Pr 30:19). Yet poets continue to craft their charming cantos, melodies of love fill the air with their beauty, and lovers continue to rejoice in both the substance and the ethereality of their rapture in each other.

WONDERFUL WORDS

So too in any discussion about God. If I wish to say something about God, then I must use words, inadequate as they may be, for without words I cannot say *anything* about him. Those words may (and do) fall far short of the divine reality, but they allow us to gain *some* understanding, and thus to enter into a closer relationship with God. (26)

That last idea is important, for knowledge of God cannot be merely an intellectual exercise; our quest must be to know **him**, not merely something *about* him. Indeed, it is impossible really to know *anything* about God without knowing the Lord himself. True, Paul does allow that the ungodly may become aware of some of God's attributes, even those that are invisible, simply by opening their eyes and looking around them –

> *All around us the created world reveals God's invisible qualities, especially his eternal power and divine nature, for these are clearly seen in what he has made. Consequently, people who deny him have no excuse. (Ro 1:20)*

But we cannot be content just to know that God exists, and that he is our Maker. Always the end of our quest must be to discover him personally and to enter into the richest possible relationship with him. To that end Christ came. To that end our studies should bring us. (27)

---

(26) One awkward limitation of language when discussing God is the necessity of describing him in masculine terms (he, him, himself, his), although God is neither male nor female. But our language offers no alternative. Some try to limit this fault either by using female pronouns instead of male, or by flipping from one to the other. But that draws even more attention to the inadequacy of both clusters of pronouns, and makes the writing clumsy.

(27) For some additional thoughts on the barriers that prevent us from fully comprehending God (or indeed, anything), see again *Addendum One* below.

WISE WORDS

The main theme of this book is the *attributes* of God. "Attribute" means the inherent characteristic or innate quality of something. In the case of God, it means those things that are an integral part of the divine being, such as love, mercy, wisdom, truth, and the three "O" words – omnipotence, omnipresence, and omniscience.

Let us at once note that these attributes do not stand apart from or below the Lord, they have no separate existence, they are not merely divine *possessions*. On the contrary, they define his very nature – for example, God does not merely *have* love, or even *show* love, he ***is*** love (1 Jn 4:8,16) – as he is also *truth, holiness, mercy,* and so on.

Hence (once again) there can be no true discovery of any of the divine attributes apart from an encounter with God himself and a developing relationship with him. Thus we cannot discuss the attributes of God with any truth if the matter is approached as an intellectual exercise, or as a piece of abstract thought. Always we are searching for God himself, not just for knowledge about him.

Mere philosophising or theologising is a hollow and barren exercise. We yearn to know the Father. And we enter this search with full understanding that we can discover nothing unless the Lord chooses to reveal himself to us, whether through nature or scripture. For the same reasons, too, we should remember the admonition of Solomon –

> *Watch your step when you go to the house of God. It is better to go there and listen than to bring the sacrifices fools bring. Fools are unaware that they are doing something evil. Don't be in a hurry to talk. Don't be eager to speak in the presence of God. Since God is in heaven and*

> *you are on earth, limit the number of your words.*
> *(Ec 5:1-2)*

To which we might add the sentiments of Uncle Toby, who "never spoke of the being and natural attributes of God, but with diffidence and hesitation". [28]

I am not ashamed to admit the same quality of diffidence in the following pages. A little more of it among Christian leaders would have prevented many blood stains from appearing on the pages of church history. Nonetheless, by revealing his attributes in both scripture and nature God has provided us with at least a partial revelation of himself. It is a revelation that falls far short of a full discovery of God, but it does disclose all that the Father intends us to know about the Godhead in this present life.

Finally (in this meditation), note that the following studies are, and must be, incomplete. There is probably no limit to the number of variations that could be added to any description of the divine attributes. How could the *infinite* God ever be comprehended within any set of propositions devised by a *finite* human mind, or even by the entire company of mankind?

> Our little systems [29] have their day;
> They have their day and cease to be;
> They are but broken lights of thee,
> And thou, O Lord, art more than they. [30]

---

(28)   Laurence Sterne, <u>Tristram Shandy</u> (1759); Oxford University Press, Oxford, 1983 edition; pg. 457 *(Volume VIII, Chapter XIX)*.

(29)   Of theology, philosophy, science, etc.

(30)   Alfred, Lord Tennyson, <u>In Memoriam</u>, lines 17-20 of the *Prologue*.

FIVE

REASONS

> Let us with a gladsome mind
> Praise the Lord for he is kind;
> For his mercies shall endure,
> Ever faithful, ever sure.
> Let us sound his name abroad,
> For of gods he is the God;
> He with all-commanding might,
> Filled the new-made world with light.
> For his mercies shall endure
> Ever faithful, ever sure. [31]

Nasr'eddin Hodja [32] was a renowned 13th century Turkish imam, preacher, scholar, and wit. In the Muslim world he has a reputation for pithy sayings akin to that in the West of the Greek slave Aesop. In one of the stories told about him, he was approached by four boys who handed him a bag of walnuts saying, "Hodja, we can't decide how to divide these walnuts among us. Will you help us, please?"

The Hodja asked, "Do you want me to divide them God's way or man's way?" At once, supposing they will get a fairer distribution, the boys cried, "God's way!" Whereupon the Hodja gave two handfuls of nuts to one boy, one handful to

---

(31) John Milton, *Let Us With a Gladsome Mind,* based on Psalm 136, and composed in 1623 when he was 15 years old; st. 1,2, & 3, with refrain.

(32) "Hodja" is a title given to a Turkish wise man, teacher, or mullah.

another, three nuts to the third, and none at all to the fourth boy.

At once the boys who were given fewer nuts protested, "What kind of division is this?"

The Hodja calmly replied, "Is this not God's way? He gives much to some people, less to others, and little or nothing to many. If you had asked me to share the nuts man's way, then I would have counted them and given an equal number to each of you."

Thus the wise man endeavoured to teach the boys the inscrutability of God, which is an idea echoed several times in scripture. (33) Therefore we should guard our speech when we speak about God and recognise that our wisest words are little better than darkness! Nonetheless, we must bravely venture, and hope to shine a little light here and there.

IS THERE A GOD?

I have read somewhere that the philosopher Sidney Hook in 1989, toward the end of his life, said that he did not believe in God, although he thought that believing in God was a good idea. He was asked what he would say if, when he died, he found himself standing before God? Hook replied, "Lord, you didn't give me enough evidence."

Is that true? Has the Lord rather irresponsibly left us without sufficient proof of his existence? Is there any proof at all?

Some of the following meditations will look at some of the evidence that God is real, but for now let me admit that no one, by rational argument alone, can "prove" the existence of

---

(33)　　Psalm 92:5; Isaiah 55:8-9; 1 Corinthians 13:12; 1 Timothy 6:16.

God. A sufficient case can be made, so that belief in God cannot be deemed absurd. But always there is enough room left for people who insist upon doubting.

In this lack of unassailable evidence we are one with the atheist. He says there is no God, but cannot prove it. We say there is a God, but cannot prove it. (34) However, there is certainly enough proof to make belief in God sensible, and some good arguments can be raised in favour of theism against atheism. The renowned French mathematician, physicist and philosopher, Blaise Pascal (1623-1662), created one that he thought was invincible. It is called *Pascal's Wager*, and it occupies *Meditation Seven* below. Yet Pascal himself acknowledged that in the end no argument can convince someone who is resolute in disbelief. Faith in God must finally arise in the heart, not the mind. As he said –

> *"The heart has its reasons, which reason cannot know!" And again, "It is the heart, not reason, that experiences God." This then is faith: God perceived by the heart and not by reason.* (35)

Paul, though, held a rather stronger view. He insisted that what can be known about God should be plain to all people, because God has shown it to them. His invisible attributes, such as his eternal power and divine nature, have been clearly displayed since the creation of the world. They are revealed in the natural world all around us, so that unbelievers have no excuse (Ro 1:19-20). Yet even Paul would allow that only faith, itself a gift from God, can show

---

(34) See the following meditation and my book Strong Reasons.

(35) Pensees # 277, 278; E. P. Dutton & Co. Inc, New York; 1958.

us that God is love, and that he has acted in Christ to rescue us from our folly and to bring us into his eternal family.

And it is well that we *can* trust the impulse of our hearts toward God, for without it the human condition is unbearable. On the one hand I sense that I am greater than the universe, because I am aware that it exists, and in my mind I can encompass its vast grandeur, travelling instantly to the furthest reaches of space. On the other hand, I am compelled to admit that the universe has no knowledge of me, and is utterly indifferent to my existence. Worse, I am obliged to recognise my helplessness beneath the crushing forces of nature! Wind and wave, fire and flood, destroy humans mindlessly and pay no heed to our cries. We alone lament our ruin. We alone know that we are being ruined. The universe, without soul, without mind, is without knowledge of our fate, and remains unmoved by it.

Similarly, we are so wise in many things, yet we search for ultimate truth in vain. We can say *how* things happen, but seldom, and ultimately never, *why*. A candle burns yellow, and physicists can tell us in marvellous detail what processes are at work. But *why* those chemical reactions should always produce that result, and not another, lies beyond the skill of the wisest person who ever lived, for it is hidden within the primeval decree of God.

Pascal defined our anguish as not being able to validate what we believe, yet equally unable to yield to scepticism. Torn between the two, we cannot resolve either of them. We sense within ourselves an extraordinary nobility, yet it is matched with a capacity for awful debasement. We are at once the quintessence of beauty and of ugliness, of infinite value yet no value, sensing ourselves immortal yet doomed to perish. We know everything and nothing, we *are* everything and nothing, all at the same time.

In the end, peace comes only from surrendering to the grace of God in Christ. In him we discover who we truly are, and our eventual destiny in Paradise. Christ gives meaning and value to everything in such a way that we cry with Paul –

> the sufferings of this present time are not worth comparing with the glory that will be revealed in us! *(Ro 8:18)*

Indeed, although creation may presently be *"subjected to futility"*, and so lie in bondage to death and decay, it will be set free on that great day when the children of God are revealed in all their incandescent magnificence (vs. 19-21; 1 Th 1:7-8).

But who is this God who changes everything? What does he do? What is his nature? How does he exist? How shall we describe him?

Can such questions even be answered? In some ways, yes; in other ways, no. The quest is an exciting one and will take us into a realm where eventually finite words will fade away in the presence of the infinite. But we will travel as far as we can and learn something, even if it falls far short of everything.

But perhaps we have jumped into this discussion too soon. Perhaps the first thing to establish is the very existence of God. For if there is no God, then any talk about his attributes is a piece of fiction, about as useful as talking about the attributes of green men from Mars.

That question will occupy my next meditation.

40

SIX

TREES

> I think that I shall never see
> A poem lovely as a tree.
> A tree whose hungry mouth is prest
> Against the sweet earth's flowing breast;
> A tree that looks at God all day,
> And lifts her leafy arms to pray;
> A tree that may in summer wear
> A nest of robins in her hair;
> Upon whose bosom snow has lain;
> Who intimately lives with rain.
> Poems are made by fools like me,
> <u>But only God can make a tree</u>. (36)

Is it true, that only God can make a tree? What about evolution? What about the Big Bang? Can we even be sure that God exists?

For a Christian, of course, the resurrection of Christ settles the matter beyond dispute. Jesus came. He died. He rose again. He ascended into heaven and took his seat at the *"right hand of the Majesty on high"* (He 1:3). His testimony concerning the Father, that he is the Maker of all things, removes all doubt from a believer's mind.

Still, even for us, questions about evolutionary theory remain. Can God and evolution co-exist? Some people, of course, speak a forceful "No!" and they sternly reject God

---

(36)   Joyce Kilmer (1886–1918); *Trees*.

and embrace evolution. Others just as furiously reject evolution and embrace God. For myself, I prefer a more neutral stance. I am not a palaeontologist, biologist, chemist, nor a scientist, and I am reluctant to pass judgment on matters about which I know little. I have only such knowledge of things scientific as any intelligent layman may accumulate over the years. Nonetheless, I have looked at the evidence both for and against the *theory of evolution*, and find that I can accept evolution as a theory of <u>*process*</u>, but hardly as a theory of <u>*origins*</u>. It may tell us many useful things about how the various species developed, but it can say nothing at all about the <u>*ultimate origin*</u> of all things.

Similarly, the Big Bang (supposing it actually happened) suffers from its inability to explain the <u>real</u> beginning of the universe, even if that was only a "point of singularity" (as some physicists call it). Whatever the source of the Big Bang, there was still a *source*, which it cannot explain. But the Bible can, and does. It simply says that *"in the beginning God created the heavens and the earth"* (Ge 1:1). God spoke, and all that presently exists began to come into being. That was indeed a big bang!

But my neutrality is affronted when evolutionists go beyond physics into metaphysics and try to argue that their theory obviates the need for a Creator. When a secular theory is presented as a "scientific" explanation of the <u>*existence*</u> of the universe it travels wildly past its proper boundaries. If it is fair to offer evolutionary theory such credibility then creationists have every right to demand equal time. That is because when it comes to *origins*, evolution has nothing "scientific" to say more than any other theory.

WHY IS THAT THE CASE?

On the question of where the universe came from, the choice is between an eternally self-existing, uncaused *world*, or an eternally self-existing, uncaused *God*.

Neither proposition can be "scientifically" proved, and neither of them should be part of a college science class. They belong in the realm of metaphysics, not physics.

Is evolution then wholly false or unprovable?

There seems little reason to question the claims that evolutionists make about developments both within and across various species. The available evidence for evolutionary development seems to me quite strong. That is, once again, evolution as a theory of *process* for at least some aspects of the development of living things, seems to have sufficient supporting evidence. But only *some*. One look at a baby and I cannot by any stretch of imagination accept that such a collection of miracles just evolved by chance. And certainly, evolution as a theory of *origins* cannot speak any more reliably than any other theory.

Indeed, neither *evolutionism* nor *creationism* can have anything *scientific* to say about the *origin* of the universe, because it is a matter that lies beyond any scientific test or experiment.

TWO DIFFERENT TEXT BOOKS

The Christian Bible and the Scientific Textbook should not be viewed by Christians as antagonistic towards each other. Rather, each should be seen as a different perspective on the same ultimate truth, which is reflected in the created universe.

The Bible is not a Science Textbook; the Science Textbook is not a Bible. That is to say, the Bible has nothing to say that is strictly _scientific_, but instead deals with the spiritual concerns of humankind – what is the true nature of human life and our eventual destiny; and what is the quality of our existence as we reach towards that destiny. (37)

On the other hand the Science Textbook has nothing to say about the _philosophical_ or _spiritual_ concerns of humanity. Science is (or should be) concerned solely with delineating the probable nature of the world around us. It deals with the material, not the immaterial. Its realm is the mundane, not the heavenly. It is wrapped within the confines of time and cannot reach into eternity. It touches the dominions of mankind, it cannot span the realm of God. It is flesh, not spirit; earth, not soul; the instrument, not the song.

I do not mean that those two sources, the Bible and Science, cannot influence each other. In a perfect world they would mesh in ways that complement and enrich each other. Unfortunately what more often happens is that proponents of each school of thought try to encroach upon the other's areas. Thus, even though the Bible is not a Textbook, and the Textbook is not a Bible, one constantly finds scientists making ignorant statements about religion and theologians making ignorant statements about science. That is as ridiculous as an artist performing surgery on a slipped disk, or a surgeon installing the electrical wiring of a skyscraper!

---

(37)   I am aware that Muslims would claim for the Koran what I am asserting of the Bible, as would other faiths for their sacred texts. But I accept the divine inspiration and authority of the Bible, above all other books, and cannot enter here into proof of that assertion.

So both theories (scientific and biblical), when they talk about *origins*, move away from science and into metaphysics – they turn from demonstrable fact to pious dogma.

LOCKED INTO A SYSTEM

We cannot in this world discover anything final about it because we are locked into it and bounded by it. Gödel conclusively demonstrated (1931) that while one is still standing inside any system, no <u>absolute</u> proof can be offered for anything. [38] To do that, one has to step outside the system (which for us is impossible). Therefore every scientist has to accept the truth of many axioms that cannot be proved. As Paul Davies wrote –

> However successful our scientific explanations may be, they always have certain starting assumptions built in. For example, an explanation of some phenomenon in terms of physics presupposes the validity of the laws of physics, which are taken as given. But one can ask where these laws come from in the first place? One could even question the origin of the logic upon which all scientific reasoning is founded. Sooner or later we all have to accept something as given, whether it is God, or logic, or a set of laws, or some other foundation for existence. Thus 'ultimate' questions will always

---

(38) By "absolute proof" I mean proof that is free from any prior assumptions, pre-suppositions, or prejudices. That is, proof that can stand entirely by itself, not being contingent upon any other thing.

lie beyond the scope of empirical science as it is usually defined. (39)

And again –

> It seems to me that, if one perseveres with the principle of sufficient reason and demands a rational explanation for nature, then we have no choice but to seek that explanation in something beyond or outside the physical world – in something metaphysical – because, a contingent physical universe cannot contain within itself an explanation for itself. (40)

We Christians of course declare that Someone who *does* stand outside the boundaries of our physical universe *has* spoken to us, telling us the truth about things that otherwise we would never have known. We find his story in the Bible, which describes many things that lie beyond the realm of space and time, far out of the reach of human research.

THE GREAT DEBATE

In the end (unless one is a determined solipsist (41), all the quarrels about origins must resolve to the one indisputable fact – *the universe exists*.

---

(39) Op. cit.; pg. 170-171.

(40) Ibid. pg. 171.

(41) "Solipsism" comes from the Latin solus (alone) and ipse (self), and is the name of a doctrine that each human mind has no ground upon which to believe in anything except its own existence. As Descartes said, "I think, therefore I am." But beyond that I cannot prove whether or not the images, experiences, etc, that beset me each day are real or merely products of my own imagination. In practice, of course, whether
... *continued on next page* ....

From that point there are two options –

- the universe is eternally self-existent; or
- the universe is the work of a creator.

Neither statement is susceptible to "scientific" proof, for both are *statements of faith*. But which is more rational, indeed, easier to believe –

- that all things exist, including intelligence, as a product of forces with no intelligence? Or –
- that all things were called into being and for a purpose by an infinitely wise and powerful Creator? (42)

So we find this odd situation – one person says that God does not exist; but he cannot "prove" it, while another says that God does exist; but neither can he "prove" it. Neither party can claim scientific proof because, once again, both positions are statements of faith. I suppose, too, that a real sceptic could no more be an *atheist* than a *theist*, for his scepticism should cause him to doubt atheist dogma as much as he scorns the theist version. But many atheists, with an astonishing disdain for integrity, boldly assert that their view alone is rational and is supported by empirical evidence. But what evidence? How can the existence, or non-existence, of an eternal, invisible, almighty deity, ever rest upon some handful of dust gathered on this infinitesimal speck we call Earth?

---

        or not we can "prove" that the outside world exists, we behave as if it does, for to do otherwise courts insanity.

(42)   For more on this, see *Addendum Two* below, *"The Cosmological Argument."* I might add, too, that I was rather pleased with the above formulation when I first conceived it, only to discover later that countless other writers had got there before me!

But we Christians have at least this advantage – once we come to faith in God we have no difficulty in seeing abundant confirmation of the Creator's design in a thousand ways every day! The Christian position, too, does have the merit of fitting readily within our ordinary mindset – that is, when we see an *effect* we instinctively look for a *cause* and we are deeply doubtful of any claim that a cause either cannot be found or does not exist. If that is true in small matters, then how much more must it be true in matters universal! If I see a splash of paint on a wall, I say that a painter must have been careless. If I see a planet, a cluster of planets, a galaxy, a universe, how can I imagine that it just happened? Such an astonishing effect surely demands a sufficient cause!

For that reason, theism is a more natural and instinctive belief than atheism. Indeed, it takes considerable mental effort to become and to remain a truly committed atheist, whereas even little children easily accept the existence of God and pray to him with simple faith. Indeed, because atheism defies both our common reason and our ordinary instincts, most people find it difficult to join with atheists in scoffing at the very idea of God. It is far easier to believe in a god, any god, even if that belief is shadowy and of little practical use. Perhaps too, there are no truly genuine atheists, which William Cummings suggested when he said, "There are no atheists in the foxholes." Atheism is an indulgence of the well-fed and prosperous. Other people need someone to thank when good things happen, and someone to trust when darkness envelops the soul.

THE ONE REASON FOR FAITH

In the end there is only one empirical reason to believe in God. All the "proofs" [43] of God finally come to this – *"Something exists, therefore God exists."* But that affirmation unquestionably remains an act of faith. That is, as we have seen, neither the atheist nor the theist positions are susceptible to indisputable empirical proof. They must be accepted or rejected on the basis of faith alone.

So it is no more an offence against reason to say that God *exists* than it is to say that he *does not* exist. In the end, reason cannot help us here, for we cannot absolutely prove or disprove the existence of God. It is finally just as much an act of faith to say, *"There is no God!"* as it is to say, *"There is a God!"* But the consequences of those two affirmations differ enormously! –

- If I **_deny_** the existence of God, I strip life of any purpose and value. Death becomes the only end and the grave, corruption, and total obliteration our only destiny.
- If I **_affirm_** the existence of God, then suddenly life takes on real purpose and measureless value. Death is no longer a thing to fear, the grave becomes only a temporary bed.

Indeed, for a Christian, the aspect of all creation is changed –

> Heaven above is softer blue,
> Earth around is sweeter green,
> Something lives in every hue,

---

(43) See <u>Strong Reasons</u>–*Part Two*. The five classic proofs of God are the *teleological; ontological; anthropological; sociological;* and *cosmological* proofs.

Christless eyes have never seen;
Birds with gladder songs o'erflow,
Flowers with deeper beauties shine,
Since I know, as now I know.
I am his, and he is mine. (44)

---

(44)   Loved with Everlasting Love, by G Wade Robinson.

SEVEN

WAGERING

> Lord of all being, throned afar,
> Thy glory flames from sun and star;
> Centre and soul of every sphere,
> Yet to each loving heart how near.
> Grant us thy truth to make us free,
> And kindling hearts that burn for thee,
> Till all thy living altars claim
> One holy light, one heavenly flame. [45]

Pascal long ago observed what many others have experienced, that there is something peculiar about the proofs of God's existence –

> The metaphysical proofs of God are so remote from the reasoning of men, and so complicated, that they make little impression. If some find them profitable, it is only during the moment that they grasp them; an hour afterwards they fear they have been mistaken. [46]

So reason by itself is inadequate to cement faith in God. And this remains true even when the biblical oracles and miracles both past and present are added to the equation –

---

(45)   O.W. Holmes (1848).

(46)   Op. cit. #381. Once again, see my book <u>Strong Reasons</u> for the classical "Proofs of God", where they are discussed in some detail.

> The prophecies, the very miracles and proofs of our religion, are not of such a nature that they can be said to be absolutely convincing. But they are also of such a kind that it cannot be said that it is unreasonable to believe them. Thus there is both evidence and obscurity to enlighten some and confuse others. But the evidence is such that it surpasses, or at least equals, the evidence to the contrary; so that it is not reason which can determine men not to follow it, and thus it can only be lust or malice of heart. And by this means there is sufficient evidence to condemn, and insufficient to convince; so that it appears in those who follow it, that it is grace, and not reason, which makes them follow it; and in those who shun it, that it is lust, not reason, which makes them shun it. [47]

Most thoughtful people come to the same conclusion – there is enough evidence of God to make belief in him quite reasonable, but not so much that no room is left for doubt. In the end, recourse must be had to the grace of God himself and to faith.

But then something wonderful happens – those who believe, *know!* Faith brings its own authentication.

Thus, I choose to respond to the gospel, to believe in God, to embrace Christ as Saviour, and at once I *know* that he is real and that I have come into a dynamic and infinitely wonderful relationship with him. Sensible argument may bring me part of the way to this discovery, but faith alone can carry me across the hiatus of uncertainty onto the solid ground of

---

(47)   Ibid. #563.

membership in the family of God. Faith alone can bring me the deepest assurance of eternal life.

"PASCAL'S WAGER"

But let us for the moment dismiss the confidence that faith brings and instead imagine ourselves to be thoughtful people trying to decide whether or not God exists.

At once we find ourselves facing a problem – none of the arguments for God's existence are conclusive. But then, none of the arguments *against* his existence are conclusive either. So we are bound to say – since there are good arguments for both positions – that logical reasoning by itself cannot finally prove nor disprove God's existence. Yet there is hardly a more important issue to resolve! If God exists, if he is truly my Maker, then he rightly deserves my loyal service, love, and trust. It becomes a criminal act to mock his glory and to despise his commands. But if God does *not* exist, then what folly it is to waste a whole life in worshipping, serving, and sacrificing for him!

Can we resolve this dilemma?

Pascal, despite the inadequacy of reason alone to discover God, reckoned that there was one very strong argument in favour of faith. It is called today *Pascal's Wager*. He himself said of it, "This is demonstrable; and if men are capable of any truths, this is one." [48] That is, here is a reason for believing in God that seems to be unassailable. It goes like this – [49]

---

(48)   Ibid. #233.

(49)   I gleaned some of the ideas in the following paragraphs, dealing with Pascal's Wager, from Fundamentals of the Faith by Peter
         ... *continued on next page* ....

WAIT AND SEE?

Pascal asks, "Is it reasonable to wait until the moment of death to learn whether or not God is real?" Surely then it will be too late? Mere prudence would seem to demand that we lessen the risk by affirming faith in God.

Someone may respond that a choice ought not to be made either way. A neutral stance is more sensible. But that is a piece of self-delusion, for we cannot help but choose either to accept or deny that God exists. This is because we are already on the journey to the grave when it will be too late to discover that we were wrong! Whether we choose it or not, we are all involved in a wager with the future. We cannot remove ourselves from the bet. The dice have already been rolled and we must call our choice.

But is that not unjust? No, for suppose you are incurably ill and an unproved medicine is suggested that has a good chance of making you well. Would either a neutral attitude or rejection be a rational choice? Hardly! A sensible person would try the remedy, even at the risk of failure.

Or again, an unconfirmed report reaches you that your house is on fire. Would you just either ignore it or reject it? Would you not "play it safe" and act on the report?

Or again, either God is, or he is not. If I accept him, and then find at the moment of death that I was wrong, what have I lost? Except for a foolish dream of heaven, I have lost

---

Kreeft; Ignatius Press, San Francisco, 1988. Others, of course, come from the *Pensees* itself, and from a couple of additional volumes on philosophy. See also http://www.peterkreeft.com . And for *Twenty Arguments for God's Existence*, on his web page click the item More Topics.

nothing. I will simply slip all unaware into a cessation of all existence and eternal oblivion. I will not even know that I lost the wager. Along with the passing of life, all consciousness will also cease. So I am none the poorer if in fact my choice to believe should prove to be false, for I will never know that I was wrong!

But what if I reject God, and then find when I die that he exists? It will be too late to rectify my folly! I must bear the consequences of having scorned all the evidence that does indeed point towards his existence.

Given that I have nothing worthwhile to lose by believing, but may face irretrievable and awful loss if I do not believe, then atheism seems like an absurdly risky gamble.

So here is a wager where, if I win, I win everything; but if I lose, I lose nothing!

If such a wager truly does exist, and it seems that it does, then only a fool would refuse to enter it! But we have *already* entered it! None of us can avoid it. Whether we like it or not, to make a choice *against* believing in God is to risk an appalling loss.

So once again, if God does not exist then it doesn't matter what I believe, for there is nothing either to gain or lose after death. But if God *does* exist, then by not believing I squander the only chance I will ever have of eternal happiness.

WHY SUCH A PENALTY?

Why will atheism attract a dread penalty? Because if God is indeed Creator then he deserves my utmost love, obedience, worship, and trust. Therefore, failure to offer him these things is the direst crime and merits the worst punishment.

Any reasonable pondering of these things must lead to the conclusion that faith is the only safe path to take. There is nothing to lose but everything to gain by believing; but everything to lose and nothing to gain by not believing.

Further, every unbeliever should face the fact that he or she cannot be <u>sure</u> that God is a fairy tale. At the very least it must be acknowledged that God may indeed be real, even if unproven.

RISKING EVERYTHING TO GAIN NOTHING!

Someone might say that the risk is worth it because the cost of being a Christian is too high! But what does a Christian lose that is worthwhile when measured against the marvelous benefits of a Christian life? And how can I lose when I am wagering the finite on the chance of winning the infinite?

Someone else may object that *Pascal's Wager* is akin to the spurious argument that promoters of lotteries use: if you decide to buy a ticket, you have a chance at great wealth; if you don't buy it, you are certain to win nothing. Since the ratio of money given out in prizes is much less than the total collected, then buying tickets is obviously not a wise investment. It is just a plain gamble with scant chance of winning.

But the argument is fallacious, for the simple reason that I am under no obligation to purchase lottery tickets. But in the case we are considering, *we have no choice but to enter the lottery*. We are already participants and cannot opt out. We *must* wager! Yet to cast our bet one way may bring irretrievable and eternal loss, with no possible gain; while to cast it the other way, by trusting in God, may gain us eternal Paradise. Thus we can suffer no loss if we are wrong (for if there is no God, then death is the simple and absolute end of everything); but if we are right then we shall gain indescribable riches and happiness!

Of course, we have many greater and higher reasons to believe in God than a mere fear of being right or wrong. But this is nonetheless a useful starting point for faith. It provides a strong reason to believe, and it highlights the folly of deliberate unbelief. From this point, however, it would be hoped that the new believer will go on to search out much higher and nobler reasons for faith, and will enter into a genuine spiritual communion with God.

GOD IS LOVE

Reason may be enough to show the *"eternal power and glory of God"* (Ro 1:19-20), but does it prove that he loves us? The answer is both "yes" and "no" –

- "**Yes**," because the evidence all around us displays a benevolent providence, which is highlighted by these words from Joyce Kilmer's poem –

    A tree whose hungry mouth is prest
    Against the sweet earth's flowing breast;
    A tree that looks at God all day,
    And lifts her leafy arms to pray.

Or the Psalmist expressed much the same idea in his hymn –

> *How many wonderful things you have made, O Lord, and crafted them all by your own wisdom. Your creatures are scattered all over the earth. ... They all look to you to provide them with food at the right time. You give it to them, and they gather it gladly. You open your hand, and your abundance is poured out upon them. (104:24-28)*

Wherever we look, and across the entire span of human history, the story is the same – this home of ours is rich with everything we need for life, health, and happiness. Accordingly, many people have found in this unfailing supply sufficient evidence that the Maker of all is benevolent. Yet there are times when nature fails, when drought and famine, earthquake and pestilence, flood and fire, assault the land and plunge its people into misery. Does this negate the love of God? No, because people have always sensed that the world is sometimes *cruel* only because it is *sick*. The vision of the prophet echoes how people everywhere have thought the world should be –

> *The wolf will romp with the lamb; the leopard will lie down beside the young goat; the calf, the lion, and the fattened calf will live together; and a little child will lead them. (Isaiah 11:6)*

Across the ages the human heart, with a deep certainty of its reality, has yearned for the coming of this Utopia. Its ultimate arrival has been guaranteed to us by Christ (Ro 8:19-23).

Yet we must also answer –

- "**No**," because the world is sometimes ravaged by such overwhelming pain, injustice, and inequality, that any talk about a loving God sounds like mockery.

So in the end, the only sure proof we have of the love of God is found in Christ who came among us for the express purpose of demonstrating the love of God, especially by his loving sacrifice of himself on our behalf at Calvary (Jn 3:16).

And that proof is sure indeed, for no event in history is so well-attested as the life, death, and resurrection of Jesus of Nazareth. But that is another study. [50]

---

(50)   See my books The Cross and the Crown and When the Trumpet Sounds.

EIGHT

BLAME

> Fight the good fight with all thy might,
> Christ is thy strength, and Christ thy right;
> Lay hold of life, and it shall be
> Thy joy and crown eternally.
> Faint not, nor fear, his arms are near,
> He changeth not, and thou art dear;
> Only believe, and thou shalt see
> That Christ is all in all to thee. (51)

"My God, my God, why have you forsaken me? Why do you stay so far away? How can you listen to my desperate cry, and not rush to help me?" (Ps 22:1)

Great tragedies in human life always stir up the bitter question: "If God is truly all-powerful and all-loving, how can he allow such things to happen? Why does he not intervene to stop them?"

Indeed, this is probably the only genuine argument that atheists can raise against the existence of God. If God is able to prevent awful tragedies, yet fails to do so how can he be called loving? Or if he is truly loving, and does not prevent terrible pain, then he cannot be all-powerful. Does not even human justice oblige people, if they are able to do so, to rescue each other from threatening peril? Why then should we allow God the freedom to gaze upon injustice, cruelty,

---

(51)   J.S.B Monsell (1860), st. 1 & 4.

war, and uncountable horrors but do nothing to prevent them? Should he not have turned the Titanic away from the iceberg? Should he not have prevented Hitler from gaining power? How can he ignore tens of thousands of children dying miserably of starvation in Africa? Why doesn't he send rain? Doesn't he hear the screams of men and women being torn apart in some ghastly torture chamber? Why doesn't he intervene to prevent such foul injustice, such unspeakable and brutal cruelty?

Therefore, says the unbeliever, either there is no God; or if there is, he must either be indifferent to human affairs or lack the strength to intervene.

The problem is not new. More than 20 centuries ago biblical writers were expressing their bewilderment over divine inaction –

- sometimes God seems like **a man asleep** – *"Wake up, God! Why do you keep on sleeping? Wake up and help us! Will you never stir yourself?"* (Ps 44:23); and

- sometimes like **a beaten warrior** – *"Here we are, a people called by your name. Yet you keep on behaving like someone caught unawares, or like a warrior who has lost his strength. You say that you are among us, yet you refuse to help us."* (Je 14:9)

Then, of course, there is the story of *Job*, which focuses on the question of why God so often sits serenely and silently in heaven while abominable horrors are perpetrated on earth.

The study of this problem is called *theodicy*, which is an attempt to find arguments to sustain the goodness of God despite the existence of evil, and to justify the way he chooses to act. In the Bible the issue is raised in *Job*, in several

Psalms, in portions of the prophetic writings, and curiously and quaintly in chapters three to eight of the apocryphal work *2 Esdras.* (52) Those writers all conclude that the mystery is too deep to penetrate, and that we can do no more than trust that the Lord of all heaven and earth will do what is right, and that eventually we too will recognise that he has done so.

Even ancient writers recognised that light is knowable as light only in contrast with darkness, and that all values exist in dependence upon their contrast –

> Those who do not believe that the world was created for God and mankind, or that human affairs are ruled by Providence, think that they are using a strong argument when they say: "If there were a Providence, there would be no evils." For they declare that nothing is less consistent with Providence than the existence of such a quantity of troubles and evils in a world which God is said to have made for the sake of man. Chrysippus, arguing against such views in the fourth book of his treatise *On Providence*, says: "There is absolutely nothing more foolish than those men who think that good could exist, if there were at the same time no evil. For since good is the opposite of evil, it necessarily follows that both must exist in opposition to each other, supported as it were by mutual adverse forces; since as a matter of fact no opposite is conceivable without something to oppose it. For how could there be

---

(52) You can easily find copies of this fascinating work on the internet.

an idea of justice if there were no acts of injustice? or what else is justice than the absence of injustice? How too can courage be understood except by contrast with cowardice? Or temperance except by contrast with intemperance? How also could there be wisdom, if folly did not exist as its opposite? Therefore," said he, "why do not the fools also wish that there may be truth, but no falsehood? For it is in the same way that good and evil exist, happiness and unhappiness, pain and pleasure. For, as Plato says, they are bound one to the other by their opposing extremes; if you take away one, you will have removed both." (53)

Modern writers on theodicy have done no better than the ancients. Every attempt to explain the problem of pain falls short of satisfaction. Some of them raise more questions than they solve! So we must accept that no answer can fully meet our demands, nor remove the mystery from pain, nor the bitterness of shattering disaster.

But some defence is possible, which allows us to maintain the wisdom and goodness of God, and to that end many fine theodicies have been written. (54) I have no intention of replicating them here. Yet a book on the divine attributes cannot ignore the subject, for God is quintessentially Love, and the ongoing existence of pain and of evil do call that love into question. We might describe this as the divine attribute

---

(53) Aulus Gellius, The Attic Nights, *Bk. VII, Ch. One;* tr. J. C. Rolfe; Loeb Classical Library, 1927. Aulus Gellius was a Latin writer who flourished in Rome during the second century of our era.

(54) An excellent introductory study can be found in my brother's book, Walking with a Limp, by Barry Chant; Openbook Publishers, Adelaide; 2002.

of **_silence_** or of **_inaction_**. So I offer the following thoughts –

GOD KNOWS ALL ABOUT IT

No earthquake, flood, famine or any other disaster, ever takes God by surprise. So, why doesn't he prevent them, or at least give adequate warning?

We don't know, for many things are hidden from our eyes. But remember that Jesus predicted such things, and was able to accept them without condemning the Father –

> *You will hear of wars and rumours of wars. Don't be alarmed! These things must happen, but they don't mean that the end has come. Nation will fight against nation and kingdom against kingdom. ... There will be terrible earthquakes, famines, and dreadful diseases in various places. Terrifying sights and miraculous signs will come from the sky. (Mt 24:6-7; Lu 21:11, GW)*

Plainly, Christ saw no conflict between such horrifying events and his teaching about the love of God. He boldly declared that God cares deeply for each of his children, so that it is foolish for us to worry about what we will eat or drink, or how we will live (Mt 6:25-34). He never doubted that

- we can trust divine providence; and that
- the Father will never forsake his children; and that
- God is in full control of every event; and that
- nothing can happen, not even horrible injustice, without divine sanction (Jn 19:11).

I do not mean that terrible things are ordained by God, but only that unless he in some way allows them they cannot happen. As scripture says, *"he does whatever he pleases, in heaven and on earth"* (Ps 135:6). This is indeed a biblical paradox – how God can choose seldom to intervene in the affairs of mankind and of nature, allowing all things to follow their chosen course, while also revealing himself as a devoted and caring Father! I don't know how to reconcile those contradictions. I know only that I am often sickened by accounts of barbarities both ancient and modern, and appalled by the natural disasters that ravage entire nations; yet at the same time, I know even more fiercely that the love of God is real, so real that in Christ and for my sake he submitted himself at Calvary to measureless anguish, brutal torture, and death.

We must remember also that in the wisdom of God we live on a violent and savage planet, with a raging inferno at its core, and a turbulent surface. Its vast energies are released without respect of person or place. That is a fact of life, which we must simply endure. Yet what the planet sometimes takes from us through flood, fire, earthquake, and famine, it returns a thousand times in sweet rain, warm sunshine, gentle winds, and abundant harvests. Its gifts exceed by far its demands. If we are grateful for earth's endless bounty (which we ill deserve) we should not complain too much about its occasional exactions.

MAN IS BORN TO TROUBLE

As surely as sparks fly upward, so all who live in this world will know trouble! (Job 5:7)

Ever since the Fall, suffering has been an inescapable part of the human condition. Thus the earth produces thorns and is subject to decay and death. Likewise, beginning with the Flood, the earth has known many disasters worse than any contemporary event. Those ancient tragedies did not impugn the integrity of the Almighty any more than a current crisis can.

Jeremiah looked upon the overwhelming disaster that had fallen upon Israel – its beautiful cities piles of smoking rubble; its chief citizens tortured and impaled; its maidens raped; its children enslaved; its inhabitants ruthlessly carried off to bondage in a far country; desolation, tears, misery, and ruin on every hand. Yet still he insisted that God is good and that his love is never-failing (see *Lamentations*). Jesus too, being fully aware of the tormented history of his people, remained undisturbed in his profound trust in God. And the same can be said also of the apostles and of all the renowned servants of God. Questions they certainly had – even Jesus, dying on the cross, cried out, *"Why?"*– and answers were lacking; but their faith remained unshaken.

Remember too, that we have never been promised immunity from trouble. We are part of human society, and must accept ill fortune along with good. Note the oracle in *Jeremiah*–

> *This is what the Lord says to Baruch, "I am tearing down what I have built, and I am uprooting what I have planted throughout the earth. <u>Why then do you look for some great thing for yourself</u>? No! You can't expect any special favours, for I intend to bring disaster everywhere," says the Lord.* (45:1-5)

If we are willing to share the benefits of a nation when it is flourishing and prosperous, we cannot complain if we are obliged to share its misery when it falls. We are neither immune from its happiness nor from its sorrows. We should not expect that when a nation is visited by tragedy God will somehow make an exception of us. Christian homes, along with those of the ungodly, are washed away in a flood, or burned to ashes in a fire, or smashed to rubble in a war. They too suffer the depredations of robbers, the ruin of a business, or the rape of their women (Mt 6:19-20). Time and chance happen to Christians as they do to everyone (Ec 9:11-12). What the Lord said to Baruch, he says to all, *"Don't look for some great thing for yourself!"*

Yet the Lord *does* rescue some, and we are all told to commit ourselves to his loving providence and to trust that his angels will protect us. To which are added a hundred more promises of care, good health, prosperity, blessing, and of divine abundance. So the paradox remains. But then paradox is the very stuff of life! And as the pirate king and his comrades showed, it can be a source of much merriment – (55)

> We tried to raise our spirits faint,
> According to our custom old,
> With quips and quibbles quaint.
> But all in vain the quips we heard,
> We lay and sobbed upon the rocks,
> Until to somebody occurred
> A startling paradox.
> A paradox?
> A paradox!
> A most ingenious paradox!
> We've quips and quibbles heard in flocks,
> But none to beat this paradox!
> A paradox, a paradox,
> A most ingenious paradox!

Perhaps, in the matter of divine paradoxes, and prior to the return of Christ, no one will ever speak more wisely than the Preacher –

---

(55)   Gilbert and Sullivan, <u>The Pirates of Penzance</u>, *Act Two.*

I have discovered the secret to a pleasant and beautiful life. It is simply this – eat, and drink, and enjoy all the good that hard work under the sun can bring you during this brief life that God has given us. That is the lot appointed to every one of us. ... After listening to every argument, I have come to this conclusion – the whole duty of man is to fear God and do what he commands. (Ec 5:18-19; 12:13)

THE MYSTERY OF JOY

There are three special things we can say about the mystery of human suffering –

1. Like Job, we will lose our questions when we finally see the glory of God (Job 40:1-5; 42:1-6). No sooner did Yahweh speak to him out of the whirlwind than Job clapped his hand over his mouth, confessed that he had already said far too much, and would not utter another word of complaint! We too, when we find ourselves standing before the blazing splendour of the Almighty will be speechless, except perhaps in praise!

2. The mystery of joy is even greater than the mystery of pain.

Thus Sir Thomas Browne (1605-1682), in his *Religio Medici*, showed 400 years ago that

> while many are obsessed with the problem of evil, and of pain, we should rather explore the equally complex problem of the existence of goodness, and of joy. (56)

The fact is, both pain and pleasure are equally inexplicable and equally undeserved. When you can tell me why any of us have the least right to laughter and happiness, and what is their source, then I will feel obligated to explain the mystery of suffering. Indeed, the former is more perplexing than the latter, for despite all its troubles, there yet remains on earth more happiness than sorrow, more laughter than tears, more gain than loss, more gentleness than violence, more peace than war, and more love than hate. This imbalance of happiness over sadness demands an explanation even more than the problem of pain requires. Yet we cannot, in this life, fully penetrate the mystery of either one or the other.

There is no more reason for darkness than there is for light, nor any more reason for joy than there is for grief. But light must always prevail over the dark, and eventually all sorrow will vanish in boundless joy (Is 51:11; Re 21:1-4)

Then the third thing we can say about the mystery of pain is this –

> 3. God himself has shared this valley of tears through the sufferings and terrible death of Christ, so he is not indifferent to human need, but has himself known the worst agony of pain and death. In the end, when faced with unanswerable questions about suffering, we can do no more, nor any less, than turn our eyes toward the cross, and consider the utterly undeserved

---

(56) Paraphrased from the *Introduction* by C. A. Patrides to <u>Sir Thomas Browne: the Major Works</u>, the chief of which, of course, is the great <u>Religio Medici</u>; Penguin Classics, 1977; pg. 52.

torment that Jesus endured. No one can search out Golgotha and then suppose that God doesn't care! His love is boundless. His care is infinite. He understands your pain, because he himself was tempted, and suffered (He 2:16-18).

Yet having said this, and even if I were to say much more, still a mystery remains. For there are levels of human misery experienced, say, in the torture chambers of a brutal world, or in the ravages of the wars and natural disasters that slaughter tens of thousands of men, women, and children, for which it is impossible to find any justification. We cry with Jesus, *"God, why have you forsaken us?"* And in the end must also emulate him in the trusting sigh, *"Father, into your hands I commend my spirit!"*

NIMBY

Everybody wants God to do something, but only if his interference is confined to some other place! It is the typical "not-in-my-back-yard" *(nimby)* syndrome! How loudly they would shriek and complain if the Lord decided to take control over <u>their</u> lives! Imagine the Lord asserting mastery over <u>their</u> homes, businesses, or government! They want him to interfere in the lives of other people, but would bitterly resent any attempt by God to restrict or forbid their own actions.

Do you doubt that people would angrily oppose him? Then look at how they treated Jesus when he tried to introduce the government of God. The Jews hated him, the Romans killed him, and the Greeks laughed at him! Do you really suppose that divine intervention would be any more welcome now than then?

No! They want God to stave off disaster, pain, or loss, but they resist any accounting of their own misdeeds.

How many corporate boards would accept a divine veto over their business decisions? How many parliaments wish that the Lord would take office and tell them what their policies should be? How about if the Lord decided to curtail their pleasures because of their sin? How clamorously they would protest against such "tyranny"!

How many churches, even, truly desire divine control?

And what about yourself? You are a committed Christian, but would you welcome a restraining hand on every thought, word, or deed? Do you really want the Lord visibly peering over your shoulder every moment? No, even though we love him deeply, and wish to serve him fully, most of us prefer God to remain decently distant, not too obviously controlling our affairs! In our fallen state, having the Lord too close every moment of the day would be painfully uncomfortable.

As it happens, God respects our dignity and approves our freedom, and so in general he does not tamper with human affairs, but allows people to make their own choices and to go their own way. Since this is just what they each want for themselves, they ought not to complain when he allows the same liberty to others, even when those others behave wickedly.

WE TRASH OUR OWN PLANET

When we ourselves are busily wrecking the environment and killing each other with zeal, it ill behoves us to blame God for nature's fury! By self-inflicted wars, pestilence, famine, global warming, and the like, we slaughter millions of people. Why then should the Lord suppress natural cause and effect whenever it threatens our contentment? We are, after all, happy to receive the _benefits_ of natural law, so we cannot honestly complain when that same law happens to work to our disadvantage.

Yet having said that, we must also observe that a measure of war, pain, struggle, disaster, seems to be an inescapable part of God's plan at this time. There are several reasons for this, among them I suggest the following –

- the restless energy of fallen humanity needs some kind of release.
- crisis forces people to search for and find creative solutions.
- suffering stirs up compassion and benevolence.
- tragedy compels people toward a dependence upon God.
- one disaster may serve to prevent something worse, such as a terrible war; or it may force preventive action against disease, or against some natural peril; etc.

The idea is this: unbroken peace and prosperity, health and happiness, would leave the human race enervated, dull, empty of dynamic vitality. By contrast, the present condition drives us ever onward to higher achievement.

There is an undoubted mystery here. Yet we can be sure of two things –

First, God knows what he is doing!

Second, God has **_warned_** us that the most awful **_disaster_** of all, and the most glorious **_triumph_** ever, still lie ahead of us – see *2 Peter 3:8-18* . . .

THE WARNING

"My dear friends, here is something that you should never forget – in the sight of God one day is like a thousand years, and a thousand years are like one day! So the Lord is not

tardy in fulfilling his promise, as some have said. Rather, he is patient with you, because he does not want anyone to be destroyed. Instead, he is giving time for everyone to abandon their sins. . . .

THE DISASTER

"Nonetheless, the Day of the Lord, like a thief, will come without warning. On that Day the very sky will vanish with an awful clamour, and the earth and everything on it will be destroyed. Yes, the heavens will be aflame, they will burn with fire, and the stars above will melt away in the heat. . . .

THE LESSON

"Since we know that all these things are destined for destruction, what kind of people should we be? Surely, as we wait for the Day of God, and do all that we can to hasten its coming, we should strive to be holy and we should dedicate ourselves to the service of God. . . . In the meantime, we are waiting for what God has promised: new heavens and a new earth, where only righteousness can flourish...

THE TRIUMPH

"Therefore, my friends, as you wait for that Day, do your best to be pure and faultless in God's sight and to be at peace with him. . . . Be on your guard, so that lawless people will not be able to entice you to folly, and cause you to lose your security in Christ. Rather, continue to grow in the grace and knowledge of our

Lord and Saviour Jesus Christ, to whom be the glory, now and forever! Amen!"

NINE

UNITY

> Thou, whose almighty word
> chaos and darkness heard,
> and took their flight;
> hear us, we humbly pray,
> and, where the Gospel day
> sheds not its glorious ray,
> let there be light!
> Holy and blessèd Three,
> glorious Trinity,
> Wisdom, Love, Might;
> boundless as ocean's tide,
> rolling in fullest pride,
> through the world far and wide,
> let there be light! (57)

Atheists are strange creatures, as Dr Samuel Johnson remarked more than 200 years ago –

> It has long been observed, that an Atheist has no just reason for endeavouring conversions; and yet none harass those minds which they can influence, with more importunity of solicitation to adopt their opinions. In proportion as they doubt the truth of their own doctrines, they are desirous to gain the attestation of another understanding; and industriously labour to win a proselyte, and

---

(57)   J Marriott (1813), st. 1 & 4.

eagerly catch at the slightest pretence to dignify
their sect with a celebrated name! (58)

Or again, we might ask an atheist (in the words of Tennyson) –

> Why should we bear with an hour of torture,
> a moment of pain,
> If every man die for ever, if all his griefs are in vain,
> And the homeless planet at length will be wheel'd
> through the silence of space,
> Motherless evermore of an ever-vanishing race,
> When the worm shall have writhed its last,
> and its last brother-worm will have fled
> From the dead fossil skull that is left in the rocks
> of an earth that is dead? (59)

If there is no God before whom we are all accountable, why bother with anything? –

> *I have fought with wild animals in Ephesus. But if the dead will never live again what did I gain from it? Rather let us just eat and drink, for tomorrow we die!* (1 Co 15:32; and cp. Is 56:12)

But atheism has never been acceptable to the mass of human-kind who have (at least in the western world) generally adopted one of the –

---

(58)   The Life of Sir Thomas Browne, by Samuel Johnson (1709-84)
(59)   Alfred, Lord Tennyson, *Despair*, st. 15.

FOUR MAJOR VIEWS ABOUT GOD

Christian theism has a striking quality – it comprises an amalgam of things that are true in each of the four main views about God in western society –

1. **_Polytheism_** – an unlimited number of gods. This leads to an **_anthropomorphic_** deity; that is, gods who are made in human likeness and who often ape human follies, [60] which is a reversal of the biblical assertion that we are made in the image of God. [61] Too often, though, even Christian people are prone to re-build God into their own idea of what he should be like, and how he should behave.

A modified version of polytheism is called *henotheism* (from the Greek word "one"). It holds that there is one supreme deity, but still allows room for a multitude of lesser gods. Commonly the chief god would be one chosen from the pantheon to be the tutelary deity of a particular family, tribe, or nation.

2. **_Pantheism_** – the integration of God with nature. The name comes from two Greek words that mean "everything is god". This leads to an absolutely

---

(60) Think about the mythology of the ancient world, replete with lustful, drunk, warring, and all-too-human gods, both male and female.

(61) The Bible says that we are "made in the image and likeness" of God, which means (among other things) – (a) we possess a spirit and are made for worship; (b) we possess self-awareness; (c) we have a sense of time, past, present, and future; (d) we have a sense of humour; (e) we possess a gift of language, which enables us (i) to engage in abstract thought; and (ii) to create by the spoken word. No animal possesses these attributes, and angels possess only some of them.

immanent deity, that is, one who is part of everything and is all around us at all times, inhabiting every rock and river, every tree and bush, every mountain and lake. God and nature become one, indistinguishable from each other. (62)

3. **<u>Deism</u>** – the elevation of God beyond human knowledge. This leads to a wholly ***transcendent*** deity, one who is above and indifferent to earthly happenings. He does not interfere with the working of natural law, nor perform miracles. Having set the universe in motion he then removed his hand from it and allows all things to follow their natural course. Albert Einstein, the great physicist, once expressed it this way –"I believe in Spinoza's God, who reveals himself in the lawful harmony of all that exists, but not in a God who concerns himself with the fate and the doings of mankind." (63)

---

(62)   A modified view, called "panentheism" holds that the created universe is a finite part of the infinite deity; that is, the physical world is part of God, but not wholly identical with him.

(63)   From an article by Walter Isaacson, on the Time web site www.time.com , dated 04/04/2007. Einstein's words were sent in a telegram to a New York rabbi, Herbert S. Goldstein. Baruch Spinoza (1632-1677) was a Jewish philosopher who rejected the biblical concept of a God who is actively concerned about and involved in human affairs. Spinoza, however, was nearer to pantheism than to Einstein's deism. Einstein also held to Spinoza's determinism – that is, to the belief that our actions are all predetermined, and that our belief in free will is an illusion. "Human beings," he said, "in their thinking, feeling and acting are not free but are as causally bound as the stars in their motions." But even he had to admit that he was obliged to act as if he possessed freedom of choice, and that society depended upon people being held accountable for their actions. Determinism as a philosophy may be intellectually fascinating, but as a way of life ... *continued on next page* ....

***4.* Monotheism** – there is but one sole, unipersonal God, who stands alone in universal isolation. This idea leads to a **non-relational** deity, and usually includes the kind of fatalism that was an integral part of the ancient Hebrew religion, and is still a fundamental concept in Islam.

Grasping the true elements that lie within each of those views, Christians hold the following propositions –

CHRISTIAN TRINITARIANISM

The *trinitarian* Deity taught by the church is *one God in three persons*, which creates a relationship within the Deity, avoiding the mistakes both of *polytheism* and of strict *monotheism* –

- The error of ***polytheism*** –

In a polytheistic system the many gods and goddesses can relate to each other, but only at the cost of exclusive power. Omnipotence was beyond them. For example, in Greek mythology even mighty Zeus was at the mercy of inscrutable Fate.

- The error of ***monotheism*** –

But a strictly *monotheistic* view, which obliges the deity to dwell in lofty loneliness, has its own problems. God remains all-powerful, for there are no comparable deities to contend with him, yet neither is there any equal being with whom he can relate. How then can he be deemed *perfect*? How can scripture say that he is, and has always been *Love*? (1 Jn 4:8)

---

it is disastrous! And of course, it is denied by scripture, which plainly says that each person is responsible for his or her choices and deeds.

Those problems are overcome by the reality of the Trinity. God is indeed truly one, therefore all-powerful, and without competitor; yet he exists in Three Persons – the Father, the Son, and the Holy Spirit – so that an eternal bond of love has existed, and will always exist, within the Godhead.

We see God as the Creator of all things, but not as integrated with them; thus he *is* immanent to us, but not in the *pantheistic* sense. We live, move, and have our very being in God (Ac 17:28), but he is not fused with nature, remaining always separate from the things he has made.

Likewise, we view God as gloriously enthroned in the heavens, awful in holiness, majestic in power; thus he is indeed transcendent, but not in the *deist* sense, for he remains deeply involved with all that is happening in our world.

Thus the Christian view captures the strengths of each of the major concepts of God, but discards their weaknesses.

THREE-IN-ONE

The idea of the Trinity has had a long and troubled history. Some of the Church Fathers insisted that the Son and the Holy Spirit are subordinate to the Father, not just in office, but in being. Others argued that there is one Supreme Being who manifests himself from time to time either as Father, Son, or Spirit. Some ascribed *divinity* to the Son and the Spirit, but not *deity*. Others insisted that Father, Son, and Spirit are only titles used to describe different offices, or functions, of the One God. And many other definitions of the Godhead were conceived by different divines during the early centuries of church history.

It was not until the year 381, when a great church Council was held in Constantinople, that Trinitarian doctrine reached its final orthodox form. The bishops in council resolved that the Godhead should be defined as three distinct Persons (Father, Son, and Holy Spirit) yet existing in one Being, fully equal to each other in power, wisdom, and all other attributes, differing only in the office (or function) that each has chosen to fulfil.

In effect, the bishops endorsed the Nicene Creed, which had been drawn up some 60 years earlier. In the form adopted at Constantinople it reads (in a modern English version) –

> We believe in one God, the Father, the Almighty, maker of heaven and earth and of all that exists, whether visible or invisible.
>
> We believe in one Lord, Jesus Christ, the only Son of God, eternally begotten of the Father, God from God, Light from Light, true God from true God, begotten, not made, of one Being or Substance with the Father. Through him and by him all things were made.
>
> For us humans and for our salvation he came down from heaven. By the power of the Holy Spirit he became incarnate through the Virgin Mary, and was made a man.
>
> For our sake he was crucified under Pontius Pilate, suffered death and was buried. On the third day he rose again in accordance with the Scriptures, and ascended into heaven, where he is now seated at the right hand of the Father.
>
> (From heaven) he will come again in glory to judge the living and the dead, and his kingdom will never end.

We believe in the Holy Spirit, the Lord, the Giver of Life, who proceeds from the Father and the Son. (64) With the Father and the Son he is worshipped and glorified. He has spoken through the Prophets.

We believe in one holy catholic (65) and apostolic Church. We acknowledge one baptism for the forgiveness of sins.

We look for the resurrection of the dead, and the life of the world to come. Amen. (66)

THE CREED OF CHALCEDON

Useful as the Nicene Creed was, it failed to prevent ongoing controversy. So some 70 years later, in 451, another Ecumenical Council was held, this time at Chalcedon, an ancient maritime city in what is now Turkey. A new creed was sent out by the bishops, to be a definitive statement of Christian doctrine. It laid special emphasis on Christ as the incarnate Logos, that is, the eternal living Word of God who became flesh and dwelt among us. This was because the bishops wanted to banish four heresies –

---

(64) Some versions of the creed omit the phrase "and the Son". For many centuries this phrase was a cause of much contention, especially between Roman Catholic and Eastern Orthodox Christians, but it is now generally thought neither to add to nor remove from the creed any significant idea. The matter in any case is impossible to prove, for support can be drawn from scripture for both renderings.

(65) The word "catholic" here means "universal", and does not refer to the Roman Catholic Church.

(66) Based on an ecumenical translation prepared in 1975 and adopted by many denominations.

- They rejected any suggestion that Jesus of Nazareth was a hybrid man, with a body and mind, as usual, but with some kind of divine essence replacing his human spirit. Instead, they insisted not only upon the true and full deity of Christ, but also upon his true and full humanity.
- They rejected the doctrine that the two natures in Christ required that he be two separate persons, one in heaven and one on earth, which they rightly saw as a denial of the unity of his person. They insisted that the Logos in heaven and the Man on earth were and are one and the same Person.
- They rejected the doctrine that Christ is one person with one nature. The bishops insisted that while he is indeed one person, nonetheless he certainly has two natures – a divine nature – that of the eternal Logos in heaven; and a human nature – that of the Man of Galilee.
- They rejected the doctrine that Mary was mother only of the Man, and insisted that she must be called *theotokos* = *God-bearer*. [67] If the baby Jesus was nothing more than an ordinary human child, then there is no Incarnation, we can no longer cry "Emmanuel" – "God-is-with-Us", and the entire plan of redemption is destroyed. Our very salvation

---

(67) Perhaps unfortunately, *theotokos* came into Latin not as "God-bearer", which emphasises God rather than Mary, but as "Mother-of-God", which reverses the emphasis. This slight but significant difference in rendering eventually led to the elevation of Mary in the Roman Catholic Church to a place of high veneration and to her designation as Mediatrix with (although under) Christ, the Mediator of our salvation.

> depends upon the fact that the Man who died in our place was also our God. ⁽⁶⁸⁾

So the bishops devised the following formula, which is still accepted today as orthodox doctrine by all three major branches of the church, Eastern Orthodox, Roman Catholic, and Protestant –

> Therefore, following the holy Fathers, we all agree to teach everyone to acknowledge one and the same Son, our Lord Jesus Christ.
>
> We declare that he is perfect in Godhead and also perfect in manhood, both truly God and truly man, possessing a rational soul and a body.
>
> We declare that he is of one substance with the Father as regards his Godhead, and at the same time of one substance with us as regards his manhood. He is like us in all respects, except that he is without sin.
>
> We declare that in his deity he was begotten of the Father before time began, but yet as regards his manhood he was begotten in these latter days, for us and for our salvation, of Mary the Virgin, the God-bearer.
>
> We declare that this one and the same Christ, Son, Lord, Only-begotten, must be recognised in two natures, without confusion, without

---

(68) There is a very great mystery here (as Paul acknowledges, 1 Ti 3:16), which the bishops made no attempt to explain. They did no more than set down the boundaries of orthodox doctrine, and reckoned it heresy to transgress those limits. But the mystery remains just as impenetrable to us as it was to the apostles.

change, without division, without separation. This distinction of natures is in no way annulled by their union. Instead, the specific character of each nature is preserved and comes together to form one person and one substance.

We declare that Christ is not split nor separated into two persons, but that he is the one and the same only-begotten Son, God the Word, the Lord Jesus Christ. The prophets from earliest times have so spoken of him, and our Lord Jesus Christ himself so taught us, and so also does the creed of the Fathers that has been handed down to us. (69)

Other significant creeds were developed over the centuries, including the renowned and longish *Athanasian Creed*, which was probably composed in the 5th or 6th century. (70) None of them solved every quarrel, which may well be one of the reasons why some three centuries later the simple and lovely *Apostles' Creed* was adopted.

While the *Apostles' Creed* dates from around the 8th century, its origins go back to the 2nd century, and perhaps even back to the apostles themselves. It was primarily used as a baptismal confession, and plainly has its roots in *Matthew 16:16* and *28:19*. Here it is in the form familiar to millions of church-goers throughout the English-speaking world –

---

(69) Adapted from various modern translations of the creed.

(70) If you are curious, you can easily find this creed, along with the other creeds and much commentary, on the internet. It was almost certainly not composed by Athanasius himself, but equally certainly well expresses what he taught.

> I believe in God the Father Almighty, maker of heaven and earth. And in Jesus Christ his only Son our Lord; who was conceived by the Holy Ghost, born of the Virgin Mary; suffered under Pontius Pilate, was crucified, dead, and buried; he descended into hell; (71) the third day he rose from the dead; he ascended into heaven; and sits at the right hand of God the Father Almighty; from where he shall come to judge the quick and the dead. I believe in the Holy Ghost; the holy catholic church; the communion of saints; (72) the forgiveness of sins; the resurrection of the body; and the life everlasting. Amen. (73)

Now let me conclude this meditation on the Trinity by quoting an anonymous paean to our glorious Lord –

> O praise the Lord, ye servants of the Lord,
> Into his courts your joyful homage bring;
> Ye that within his holy temple stand,
> Lift up your hands, lift up your voice and sing –
> So shall ye have the blessing from your King.
>
> He that hath made all heaven and all the worlds,
> Shall from that Zion where his saints adore
> Look down with favour, sanctify his Church,

---

(71) That is, into Hades, the abode of the dead; not "hell" as the place of punishment.

(72) That is, the gathering of the people of God in worship, in organised communities, in local churches.

(73) For an excellent explanation of the Apostles Creed see "I Believe In ...", by Brian van Deventer; Vision Publishing, Ramona CA, 2006.

Bless them that tread his sanctuary floor,
And keep them in his ways for evermore.

All glory now to God the Father's Name;
Son everlasting, glory unto thee;
And, Holy Spirit, glory thine the same;
One God eternal, blessèd Trinity,
As ever was and evermore shall be.

TEN

HARMONY

> O love of God, how strong and true;
> Eternal, and yet ever new;
> Uncomprehended and unbought,
> Beyond all knowledge and all thought!
> O love of God, our shield and stay
> Through all the perils of our way;
> Eternal love, in thee we rest,
> For ever safe, for ever blest. [74]

Our God is no mere abstract, impersonal concept, a shadow flitting through some philosophical system. Nor can he be imagined only as a cosmic force, a kind of mindless and arbitrary originator of all things, without purpose, without feelings, unrelated in any meaningful sense to his creation. If the Lord is not known personally, then he is not known at all. If there is no fellowship with him, then there is no knowledge of him.

Here lies one of the chief values of the doctrine of the Trinity. It stresses the relational aspect of the divine being; it shows that God's chief joy lies in the giving and receiving of love, and provides the only conceivable rationale for the creation, and especially for the nature of man. He made us that he might love us, and that we might return his love.

This love that God extends to his creation is simply an expression of the love that has eternally existed within the

---

(74)　Horation Bonar (1861); stanzas 1 & 6.

Godhead itself. Indeed, it is difficult to see how God can be named Love (1 Jn 4:8,16) if within the Godhead there were only one Person. In that case, prior to the creation, he could have loved only himself, which is a repugnant idea. Nor could calling the universe into being have suddenly provoked love in the Creator's heart. Loveless from eternity, it must have remained loveless through the years of time, and then on into eternity again.

But the Trinity solves these problems. Since the Godhead has always consisted of Father, Son, and Holy Spirit, love has always been the very foundation of the divine being, and, apart from holiness, remains the most essential part of God's nature and of the relationship that exists within the Godhead.

Thus the creation, and especially the making of the human race, can be seen as an expression of the love of God, and of the delight that love finds in bestowing happiness. As the *Longer Westminster Catechism* declared long ago –

Question 20: What was the providence of God toward man in the estate in which he was created?

Answer: The providence of God toward man in the estate in which he was created, was the placing him in paradise, appointing him to dress it, giving him liberty to eat of the fruit of the earth; putting the creatures under his dominion, and ordaining marriage for his help; affording him communion with himself; instituting the sabbath; entering into a covenant of life with him, upon condition of personal, perfect, and perpetual obedience, of which the tree of life was a pledge; and forbidding to eat of the tree of the knowledge of good and evil, upon the pain of death.

In other words, God's purpose in creating us was to bring happiness to us. Of course, the qualifier to that is –

Question 1: What is the chief and highest end of man?

Answer: Man's chief and highest end is to glorify God, and fully to enjoy him forever.

But let us be clear on this. While *our* chief end must be to glorify God in word and deed, and to offer him all reverence, service, and worship – and indeed we cannot find true happiness unless we do so – that is not *his* chief end toward us.

Yet many have claimed that God's ultimate purpose is only to enhance his own glory, to bring pleasure to himself rather than bliss to us, which seems to me to turn the Lord into some kind of egocentric monster. I cannot believe that love find its best focus in loving itself! No! If God is truly Love, then that Love must be directed outward, beyond itself, to another.

Initially, Divine Love found its fulfilment in the measureless love shared within the Godhead, but then it sought the joy of bestowing joy upon a multitude of children. His loving purpose is not his own aggrandisement, but our delight, so that as the psalmist cried, *"In your presence there is endless joy; at your right hand there are pleasures for ever more!"* (16:11)

Because God is profoundly personal, rich in love, warm in relationship, we are able to call him *"Father!"*, and so address him in prayer – as Jesus himself taught us to do in the *Lord's* Prayer (*"Our Father . . . "*). Those words would be pointless if "Father" had a sense less than that of a loving and caring Person, as also would be any expectation of (or even need for) mercy, pardon, prayer, fellowship, love, and the like.

But he *is* real, and in his service we find perfect happiness, along with the magic touch that transforms even the most mundane things into steps on a stairway to Paradise –

> Teach me, my God and King,
> in all things thee to see,
> and what I do in anything
> to do it as for thee.
>
> All may of thee partake;
> nothing can be so mean,
> which with this tincture, "for thy sake,"
> will not grow bright and clean.
>
> A servant with this clause
> makes drudgery divine:
> who sweeps a room, as for thy laws,
> makes that and the action fine.
>
> This is the famous stone
> that turneth all to gold;
> for that which God doth touch and own
> cannot for less be told. (75)

A HARMONIOUS GOD

A final thought on the Trinity. Among the three Persons there is never the least disagreement, disunity, dissent, or division, but all are always fully agreed in purpose and practice.

Nor was this tri-unity disturbed during the time of the incarnation and passion of Christ. During that period Jesus was separated from the Father and the Spirit *functionally*, but in his identity as the eternal *Logos* he remained *essentially* united with the Godhead and in full possession of

---

(75)   George Herbert (1633), The Elixir.

all his powers. So there was never any sundering of the Deity, nor was heaven ever left bereft of its loveliest radiance, its most ineffable beauty, its most beatific splendour.

ELEVEN

ENTHRONED

> She saw The Helper standing near
> When grief and care oppressed;
> "A Great, Big God," Who wiped the tear,
> And soothed the aching breast.
> So, in the stress of sorrows piled,
> The gloom was lifted when
> She pointed up and sweetly smiled
> "A Great, Big God; be brave, my child,
> The birds will sing again."
>
> And always some soft silver ray
> Athwart the gloom would burst
> To chase the heavy clouds away,
> When things were at their worst.
> Her "Great, Big God" would justify
> The trembling trust of men;
> For, when the cheerless night passed by,
> The sun would wink his golden eye,
> And birds would sing again. [76]

Two of the attributes of God show a remarkable contrast — his **_transcendence_** and his **_immanence_** —

---

(76) The Birds Will Sing Again, by Australian bush poet John O'Brian (a.k.a. Patrick Joseph Hardigan, 1878-1952); first and last stanzas.

A TRANSCENDENT GOD

The known universe we are told extends at least 15,000 million light years distant from earth, (77) and contains at least 200,000 million galaxies, of which our own Milky Way is one. The Milky Way is said to be an average size galaxy, which spans 100,000 light years, and embraces perhaps 200,000 million stars like our sun. (78)

If a man were to climb into a space ship and try to fly from one side of the Milky Way to the other at 125,000 kmh, his journey would take nearly 1000 million years! So, despite the science fiction writers, the chances of anyone ever reaching another galaxy are rather slim!

Even travelling at the speed of light (300,000 km per *second*) it would take our spaceman 100,000 years just to cross our galaxy. Indeed, he would need more than four years just to reach the star nearest to Earth (*Proxima Centauri*). (79)

---

(77)   A light year is the distance a beam of light travels in 12 months at a speed of 300,000 km per second = 9.5 million million km.

(78)   The numbers in this paragraph tend to keep on changing, as telescopes and methods of calculation improve. They are the best I could find at the time of writing.

(79)   Prior to the resurrection and our entrance into an entirely new state, it seems unlikely that human beings will ever escape even our own solar system. It certainly cannot be done with any of the machines presently available to us, or indeed using any kind of current technology. If it is to be done at all before Jesus comes it will have to be through some motive power we as yet know nothing about, and involving a science that no one has yet conceived. As Bill Bryson wrote in 2003, "Space is just enormous ... Based on what we know now and can reasonably imagine, there is absolutely no prospect that any human being will ever ... *continued on next page* ....

So the universe is vast beyond imagination! No wonder the Psalmist cried –

> *When I look at the sky, which you have made, at the moon and the stars, which you set in their places – what are human beings, that you think of them; mere mortals, that you care for them? (8:3-4, GNB)*

But big as it is, God is bigger!

He dwells in a dimension far beyond the parameters of this planet or even of our capacity to imagine it. No finite mind can ever comprehend an infinite God. All our thoughts are locked into measured words and limited pictures, sometimes breathtaking in their beauty and creativity, but still incapable of grasping the illimitable realm of God. Nonetheless, we can see him as terrible in power, exalted, unapproachable, glorious beyond telling, inaccessible, limitlessly high above even the mightiest and grandest of his creatures (Jn 1:18;1 Ti 1:17; 6:15-16; Is 6:1-5).

AN IMMANENT GOD

Though God has no need of this world, he is no mere passive observer of planetary events nor of human behaviour. He has not abandoned the work of his own hand, but rather fills it with his grace and glory, sustaining, guiding, controlling, replenishing all things according to his own fixed purpose.

Thus he is ever present with us, and indeed none of his creatures can escape the divine presence (Ps 139:7-12). So he

---

visit so much as the edge of our own solar system – ever. It is just too far." – <u>A Short History of Everything</u>; Doubleday, London, 2003; pg. 23.

is further away than we can imagine, yet nearer than we can dream!

In his *transcendent* splendour we worship and fear him; in his *immanent* presence we love and serve him. And because he is immanent we can discover God in three ways –

1. through observation of his **_works_** (just as we can learn much about a man or woman by looking at the things they have done or are doing); and

2. through personal **_encounters_** with God in prayer, worship, fellowship, and times of divine visitation; and

3. through his **_self-revelation_** in scripture, which is also the criterion by which all other purported knowledge of God must be judged.

We Christians should be re-discovering God in those three ways every day of our lives.

A PURPOSING GOD

A particular expression of the immanence of God is found in the biblical revelation of his **_purpose_**, which encompasses the entire creation, all humankind, and especially his church. But the wonderful thing about the purpose of God is that he is able to and does fulfil it without denying anything of the true nature of what he has created; he does not arbitrarily compel the creation (whether natural, human, or angelic) to conform to his will.

There is no higher mark of omnipotence than this – while allowing his creatures perfect freedom of choice, God still ensures that all that he has determined is and will be done.

Caedman, who is called "the father of English sacred song", and who is the earliest English poet whose name is known, expressed the irresistible majesty of God in a lively song. It is the sole surviving example of his poetry. The Venerable Bede (c. 673-735) tells the story –

> There was in (Whitby Abbey, North Yorkshire, in the year 680) a certain brother who was particularly rich in the grace of God. He often wrote pious and religious verses, especially when a passage of scripture had been explained to him. He would turn those scriptures into poetical expressions of much sweetness and humility, using only English, which was his native language. By his verses he inspired many people to despise the world, and to hunger for heaven. Others after him tried to compose sacred poems in English, but none were ever equal to him, for he did not learn the art of poetry from men, but from God. For the same reason he never could compose any trivial or profane song, but only those that held to a religious theme, and that suited his godly soul.
>
> Because he had followed a secular occupation until late in his life, he had never learned anything about versifying. Indeed, sometimes, when he was at a celebration or festival, the guests would agree to entertain each other by taking turns at performing a song. But as soon as he saw them bearing an instrument toward him he would rise up from the table, make his escape, and return home.
>
> On one such occasion, though, having gone out of the house where the entertainment was being held, he went to the stable, where he had to take care of the horses for the night. Later in the evening, after he had composed himself for

sleep, a person appeared to him in a dream, saluted him by name, and said, "Caedmon, sing some song to me." He answered, "I cannot sing! For that very reason I left the festival, and retired to this place!" But the man who talked to him, replied, "Nonetheless, you shall sing!" "What shall I sing?" rejoined he. "Sing about the beginning of all created things," said the other. Whereupon Caedmon soon began to sing verses full of praise to God. They were songs that had never before been heard, and their sense was –

Let us now praise the Maker of the Kingdom of Heaven, the power of the Creator and his wisdom, and the works of the Father of glory.

He, being the eternal God, became the author of all wonders, who first, as almighty preserver of the human race, created heaven to be a roof over our heads, and then made the earth to be our home.

That is the sense, but not the actual words that Caedmon sang in his sleep; for verses, though never so well composed, cannot be literally translated out of one language into another. Always there will be some loss of their beauty and splendour.

Awaking from his sleep, he remembered all that he had sung in his dream, and soon added many more lines in the same theme, all of them worthy of the Deity.

... Thus Caedmon ... sang about the creation of the world, the origin of men and women, and all the stories found in Genesis. He composed many verses about the liberation of the children of Israel from slavery in Egypt, and how they entered the Land of Promise. He rendered into song many other histories from holy writ. He sang about the incarnation, passion, resurrection of our Lord, and his ascension into heaven. His verses included the coming of the Holy Ghost, and the preaching of the apostles. Nor did he neglect the terror of future judgment, the horror of the pains of hell, and the delights of heaven, along with many other verses about the Divine benefits and judgments. By his songs he hoped to turn people from the love of vice, and to excite in them instead both a love for and the practice of godliness. He became a very religious man, humbly submissive to regular discipline, but full of zeal against those who behaved badly. Thus, when his days were done, he ended his life happily. [80]

So that was how Caedmon, the 7th-century illiterate cow-herder, became a monk at Whitby Abbey and composed the first piece of extant written English. According to Bede he received the gift of song miraculously, and for the remainder of his life continued to write scores of poems and hymns that brought delight to all at the Abbey and beyond. Out of all those songs, only one has survived, his renowned *Hymn to Creation* –

---

(80)　Ecclesiastical History of the English Nation, *BK. IV, ch. xxiv*; first published in A.D. 731. I have adapted the story from several different translations of Bede.

Now let us praise the Ruler of Heaven,
Let us praise the power and wise purpose of the Almighty!
Let us praise the work of the Father of Glory,
For he, the Eternal Lord, has from the beginning
wrought wonders.
As the Holy Creator,
He first created heaven as a roof,
To cover us who live on the earth.
Then as our Guardian and Eternal Lord,
He appointed this middle earth
To be our homeland.
So let us praise the Almighty! [81]

---

(81)   This is a free translation of Caedmon's Early English. Consult the internet if you wish to find recensions of the original text, literal translations, and other historical and critical data.

TWELVE

LOVE

> Speak low to me, my Saviour, low and sweet
> From out the hallelujahs, sweet and low
> Lest I should fear and fall, and miss Thee so
> Who art not missed by any that entreat.
> Speak to me as to Mary at thy feet !
> And if no precious gums my hands bestow,
> Let my tears drop like amber while I go
> In reach of thy divinest voice complete
> In humanest affection – thus, in sooth,
> To lose the sense of losing. As a child,
> Whose song-bird seeks the wood for evermore
> Is sung to in its stead by mother's mouth
> Till, sinking on her breast, love-reconciled,
> He sleeps the faster that he wept before. [82]

No creature can inflict any hurt, pain, or grief upon God apart from his own deliberate choice to enter into their sufferings. Theologians call this the **_impassibility_** of God. The word means literally "lacking in feeling", and it is used to describe someone who is incapable of any emotion or pain. Less sternly it means someone who is not susceptible to experiencing sentiment nor to suffering injury. In the case of God it holds more the latter meaning. That is, the Lord can and does experience emotion, and is subject to hurt, but only by his own choice. If he chooses not be touched by feeling or pain, then no-one and nothing _can_ touch him.

---

[82] *Comfort*, by Elizabeth Barrett Browning (1806-61).

This is another of those doctrines where it is difficult to avoid saying either too little or too much! Some have said too much, turning God into an impassive, unsympathetic, aloof, uninvolved, and distant deity. Others have said too little, reducing God almost to a state of helplessness before the impact of human rebellion. To say that the Lord cannot feel at all, is to say too much; to say that he cannot help but feel, is to say too little. The truth is in the middle there, somewhere!

At the other end of the problem, since the joy of God is already perfect, infinite, and endless, *impassibility* means that nothing can add to or diminish the pleasure of God, except as he himself chooses to rejoice, particularly in things that please him.

Thus many scholars say that the Lord is never at the mercy of his creatures for either joy or sorrow, but is moved or unmoved solely according to his own decision, or in harmony with his own decrees. He cannot be emotionally affected, nor acted upon, by anything in creation, unless he himself so chooses. Yet having spoken that more or less orthodox view, I feel a certain ambivalence. For it seems to me that if God loves, and a loved one suffers, then even *he* cannot help but grieve, nor fail to rejoice if a loved one prospers. Love that remains unmoved, unfeeling, unresponsive, no matter what is happening to the loved one, scarcely deserves the name.

CAN GOD BE UNFEELING?

It is commonly said that divine *impassibility* does not mean that God is *impassive* or *unfeeling*, but just that neither divine laughter nor tears can be held hostage to human behaviour, nor can he ever be surprised by any event, caught unawares, and thus obliged to react in one way or another.

But can that really be true?

Difficult though it is to imagine God as subject to my behaviour, it is even more difficult to suppose that he can, while remaining true to himself, disregard what I am doing or what is being done to me. If God in his very essence truly is love, grace, mercy, truth, justice, and the like, then he *cannot* refuse to respond to things that are happening in his creation. To choose to remain indifferent to what is happening to his children, he would have to deny himself, and that is the one thing he *truly* cannot do (2 Ti 2:13).

I do not mean that God's responses must be immediate, or must take a certain form, or must agree with human expectations, but just that he *must* respond, he cannot choose to remain unmoved. If he were to do so (which it appears that he cannot do), then all those gracious attributes we have been exploring would become empty syllables, mere collections of letters.

So to the extent demanded by his own character and attributes, it would seem that God is indeed a prisoner of human behaviour.

Nonetheless, the full ramifications of the interaction between heaven and earth must remain – at least on this side of the resurrection – a mystery, and I do not wish to speak too strongly one way or the other.

But I do resist any attempt to say (as some of the old catechisms did) [83] that impassibility requires God to be void of any passion, feeling, or capacity for emotional change. They did this, because they felt that any change of any sort in God had to be either for better or worse. They reckoned that

---

(83) From the original Thirty-Nine Articles of the Church of England – "There is but one living and true God, everlasting, without body, parts, or passions." (The underline is mine.)

such changes would be contrary to his *perfection* and *immutability*, and therefore could not be allowed. It seemed to them, for example, that the perfection of bliss that fills the Godhead would be destroyed if grief should ever be allowed to darken it. Indeed, does not scripture say that God is unchangeable? (Mal 3:6; He 13:8)

But those dogmas fail to reckon with the idea that perfect happiness cannot exist apart from the possibility of sorrow. God is Love, and as I have said, love feels – not only happiness in the joy of the beloved, but also sorrow in the pain of the beloved. Love emotionally responds to the emotional state of the beloved, and it cannot help but so respond. In any case, scripture constantly depicts the Father expressing joy, sorrow, pleasure, anger, love, hate, even grief and pain. As the Lord himself says, *"I make both light and darkness; I make both happiness and sorrow. I do all these things. I am the Lord"* (Is 45:7; see also Ec 7:14). Or consider the fierce passion in these words –

> *See now that I, even I, am he, and there is no god beside me; I kill and I make alive; I wound and I heal; and there is none that can deliver out of my hand. For I lift up my hand to heaven and swear, "As I live forever, if I sharpen my flashing sword and my hand takes hold on judgment, I will take vengeance on my adversaries and will repay those who hate me. I will make my arrows drunk with blood, and my sword shall devour flesh – with the blood of the slain and the captives, from the long-haired heads of the enemy." Rejoice with him, O heavens; bow down to him, all gods, for he avenges the blood of his children and takes vengeance on his adversaries. He repays those who hate him and cleanses his people's land. (De 32:39-43, ESV).*

Those are hardly the words of a detached, dispassionate deity! No doubt there is a measure of anthropomorphism [84] in such portrayals. Yet there are so many of them, and they are often so colourful, so dramatic, that it is difficult not to credit them with at least some reality. God loves passionately, but as a necessary corollary he also hates furiously! (Ps 5:5; 45:7; Pr 6:16; Is 61:8; etc., KJV). It is as true of God as it of us that *"there is a time to love, and a time to hate, a time of war, and a time of peace"* (Ec 3:8). Indeed, if God is truly perfect, then his nature must comprehend all that exists, whether light or dark, good or evil, joy and grief, life and death, anger and peace, and so on.

So much is it true that God is deeply affected by human need, he sent his one and only Son to take on our form, and to suffer and die in our stead. That is not the action of an apathetic deity, but of one who is profoundly sympathetic with our condition and yearns to rectify it. He does as he enjoins us to do – weeps with those who justly weep, and rejoices with those who justly rejoice. Nor is there anything logically improper in this. Divine perfection does not preclude change any more (as someone has said) than a "perfect" clock is precluded from showing a different time at different points in the day. The clock "changes" with the passing hours, yet its perfection as a timekeeper is not lessened.

Now a clock is not God, and it needs to be "perfect" in only one thing, whereas God is perfect in every respect. So the illustration is perhaps a poor one. Yet its central truth

---

(84) That is, attributing human behaviour or character to that which is not human – such as God; the gods of myth and legend; animals in fables and stories; even inanimate things like the sun, moon, or earth when they are described as thinking, speaking, or consciously acting.

remains, that "perfection" can be imagined in a way that does not require a state of inertia. In other words, the assumption that all change must be either toward improvement or decay, is plainly false. Indeed, like the clock, there are many instances where perfection *requires* a capacity to change, adapt, adjust, and the like. In such cases, change does not effect the slightest diminution of value, truth, beauty, or virtue.

Further, it is difficult to see how we could have any kind of meaningful relationship with an impassive deity, one who was incapable of entering into, or sharing our laughter and our tears, our triumphs and our sorrows, our defeats and our victories. Therefore any true definition of impassibility has to take a shape something like I have suggested above. God cannot be *apathetic* but must know the full dimensions of true *pathos* – what value can there be in love without sacrifice, or love that cannot feel? Indeed, we may allow any change in God that neither diminishes nor interferes with any of his essential attributes, for our God is not static, aloof, indifferent, unmoved, but truly *alive*, and with a capacity for the emotions that we, made in his image, experience.

A LOVING GOD

So, despite the inadequacy of every definition of God, we can assert this much – God cannot do other than love all that he has made, [85] for love is the essence of his nature. This love displays itself in universal goodwill and unfailing faithfulness

---

(85)   But always remember that divine love cannot abrogate the demands of divine justice, nor the penalties that heaven's justice sometimes demands. Hence the gospel, that although God dearly loved the world, his broken law had to be requited, so he sent his Son to redeem the world.

in all his dealings with mankind, and most of all in the coming and passion of Jesus. In the Cross we find the only possible answer (in this life) to the mystery of undeserved pain, of injustice, of heaven's silence in the presence of unspeakable barbarity on earth (see Ro 8:31-39).

> Strong Son of God, immortal Love,
> Whom we, that have not seen thy face,
> By faith, and faith alone, embrace,
> Believing, where we cannot prove. [86]

---

[86] Alfred, Lord Tennyson, <u>In Memoriam</u>, Stanza One of the *Prologue*. Cp. John 20:29.

THIRTEEN

HOLINESS

> High in the heav'ns, eternal God,
> Thy goodness in full glory shines;
> Thy truth shall break through every cloud
> That veils and darkens Thy designs.
>
> Forever firm Thy justice stands,
> As mountains their foundations keep;
> Wise are the wonders of Thy hands;
> Thy judgments are a mighty deep.
>
> Life, like a fountain, rich and free,
> Springs from the presence of the Lord;
> And in Thy light our souls shall see
> The glories promised in Thy Word. [87]

The love of God is tempered by his holiness and justice, which are also absolute and eternal. Indeed it could be said that the greatest attribute of God, the one most emphasised in scripture, is not Love but *Holiness*. Therefore he cannot condone nor pass over sin, but must and does call into judgment all that offends his divine law and character.

This holiness alone will provide a sufficient condemnation of all that is unholy, unless it is cleansed by the Cross. No other judgment will be necessary, nor will any hiding place be possible, for God's holiness like a brilliant light will bring

---

(87) Isaac Watts, <u>The Psalms of David</u>; 1719; *High in the Heav'ns*, st. 1, 2, 6.

into glaring relief all that men and women prefer to hide in darkness (Jn 3:19).

Had the Father been motivated by love alone, then he could simply have pardoned our wrongdoing without the necessity of Calvary. Jesus need not have suffered so bitterly and died so terribly. But the holiness of God demanded satisfaction. The offended law of heaven had to be requited. Punishment had to be borne, either by the offenders or by an acceptable surrogate. Divine Love and divine Holiness both had to be satisfied. The death of Jesus met all the demands of Law; our rescue and salvation met all the demands of Love. A complete redemption was achieved, and joy broke forth in heaven and on earth.

This great salvation, however, must have remained forever unknown if it were not also true that our God is –

A REVEALING GOD

God does not hide himself, but reveals himself to us in three ways, each of them essential to the process of salvation.

THROUGH <u>NATURAL</u> REVELATION

See *Psalm 19:1-4; Romans 1:19-20.*

The world around us, the starry sky at night, all the marvels of creation, talk to us every day, and show us the eternal power and glory of God. Because of that, as Paul says, those who refuse to believe are left without excuse. (Ps 19:1-4a; Ro 1:20)

Most people who come to Christ have felt the impact of nature – an achingly beautiful sunset; the thrilling roar of a storm; a baby's clutching finger; a child's laughter; the sweet pangs of love; the ineffable loveliness of a fragrant rose – these and many other awesome things have compelled them to look for their Creator. That such mysteries should just happen to *be*, without cause, without reason, without purpose, without destiny, simply seems absurd. So they see, and they look, and they find God.

Yet in the end, natural theology, untaught by revelation, cannot reveal the loving character of God, and indeed may lead one to suppose him a very capricious Deity. Thus in his poem *Caliban Upon Setebos*, Robert Browning tells the story of Caliban and how one day he was meditating upon his brutal god, Setebos, and the vagaries of life –

> Thinketh, such [88] shows nor right nor wrong in Him,
> Nor kind, nor cruel: He is strong and Lord.
> Am strong myself compared to yonder crabs
> That march now from the mountains to the sea;
> Let twenty pass, and stone the twenty-first,
> Loving not, hating not, just choosing so.
> Say, the first straggler that boasts purple spots
> Shall join the file, one pincer twisted off;
> Say, this bruised fellow shall receive a worm,
> And two worms he whose nippers end in red;
> As it likes me each time, I do; so He. [89]

---

(88) That is, all the parts of nature and the vicissitudes of life.

(89) Robert Browning (1864). Caliban is one of the main characters in William Shakespeare's play *The Tempest*. Only a few lines from the middle section of Browning's poem are quoted above. The poem is sub-titled "Natural Theology in the Island". It is one of a series of poems that Browning wrote, marked by his grief at the death of his much-loved wife, Elizabeth. In them he made a "searching examination of the relation of human to divine love, especially as it concerns the nature of belief" (The Oxford Companion to English Literature, art. *Dramatis Personae* [the title of the series]; Oxford University Press, 1985). In the end, Browning's devout Christian faith remained unbroken.
... *continued on next page* ....

Browning was not the first to make such observations. The Preacher was well ahead of him, for the greater part of *Ecclesiastes* deals with the "vanity" of life, its injustice and disparity, its inequality and imbalance –

> *Consider what God has done! Who can straighten what God has bent? When times are good, be happy. But when times are bad, consider this: God has made the one time as well as the other so that mortals cannot predict their future. I have seen it all in my pointless life: Righteous people die in spite of being righteous. Wicked people go on living in spite of being wicked. I saw something else under the sun. The race isn't won by fast runners, or the battle by heroes. Wise people don't necessarily have food. Intelligent people don't necessarily have riches, and skilled people don't necessarily receive special treatment. But time and unpredictable events overtake all of them. No one knows when his time will come. Like fish that are caught in a cruel net or birds caught in a snare, humans are trapped by a disaster when it suddenly strikes them. (Ec 7:13-14; 9:11-12, GW; and the same theme is echoed in many Psalms and in Job.)*

Many a fist has been shaken at heaven when fate hands out its unpredictable and capricious dole. Life is dismally unfair, and it is impossible to explain why some should have so much, even when it is utterly undeserved, while others

---

Remember too the story about the Hodja that begins meditation Four above.

should have so little, despite unbroken virtue. So we find ourselves driven from the contemplation of nature to discover how God has shown himself –

THROUGH <u>BIBLICAL</u> REVELATION

That is, God speaks to us through the pages of scripture. The face of God is mirrored in those sacred pages. The voice of God sounds again and again. He is walking through the Bible as he walked through the Garden of old, calling us to heed him (Ge 3:8-9). But there are many who look at the Bible, yet do not see; they listen to its words, yet do not hear; they understand its pages, yet do not believe. Something more is needed. So God also reveals himself –

THROUGH <u>PERSONAL</u> REVELATION

See *Job 33:14-18*; and cp. *4:12-16*.

Always the divine intention is not that of encouraging man to begin with himself and to think through to God; but rather, to begin with God and to think through to the truth about himself! The first leads to gods made in the image of man; the second leads to the realisation that we are made in the image of God. This is the great weakness of all philosophical approaches to religion. They tend toward the glorification of the human mind, or toward giving higher authority to human speculation than to divine revelation.

I will admit that it is difficult for any theologian (myself included) to keep strictly to scripture. The subject is so fascinating that the temptation to think beyond the Bible is almost irresistible. This tendency is boosted by scripture itself, because of the incompleteness of so many biblical ideas. Few if any doctrines in the Bible are spelled out sufficiently to satisfy the questing mind of the theologian – especially scholars who are addicted to *systematic* theology, who loathe loose ends or dogmatic cul-de-sacs, who want every doctrine to be wholly coherent and comprehensive, fitting neatly with all other doctrines.

Whenever I peruse church history I am amazed all over again at how fiercely people quarrelled with and persecuted each other over dogmas that are less than well defined in the Bible. A little humility would have been more useful! And it would have been more godly to respect alternative viewpoints that are honestly held and have at least some biblical support.

Think about water baptism, church government, the eucharist, the second coming of Christ, and many other doctrines. They all contain enough room for people of good will to pick up their Bibles and come to different conclusions. Surely twenty centuries of argument have demonstrated the futility of striving to persuade everyone to accept a single interpretation of scripture, or a single body of doctrine!

The simple fact remains – always our knowledge of God must remain partial, limited, prone to error, falling short of a discovery of all that is in the Father's mind. Neither in time nor eternity will the glory of the Almighty be fully comprehensible to our minds. After all, God is *boundless*, and must forever lie beyond the grasp of a *bounded* mind. Though we search him out across eternity to come, he will always remain more hidden than revealed (1 Ti 1:17; 6:16).

It is said that Martin Luther was once pestered by a young man who constantly questioned where God had been before the world was created. Luther eventually gave an irritated reply – "He was building hell for such presumptuous, fluttering, and inquisitive spirits as you are!" The great reformer was saying that some things lie beyond enquiry, that we must be content not to know, and simply to trust in the wisdom and grace of God.

Thus also, more than two millennia ago, a wise rabbi wrote –

Our God lives for ever and he is the Creator of the whole universe. Absolute truth belongs to the Lord alone. No human will ever comprehend all the mystery of his great work, nor penetrate his wonders to their source. No one will ever tell the boundaries of God's infinite power; even less will anyone place a limit upon his inexhaustible mercy. No human can either increase or lessen the grace of God, nor will anyone ever measure the wonders of the Lord. When someone thinks he has reached the end of them he will find himself still at the beginning, and when he has done thinking about them he will still be perplexed! (Sir 18:1-7).

120

FOURTEEN

POWERFUL

> The firmament on high,
> With all the blue ethereal sky,
> And spangled heavens, a shining frame
> Their great Original proclaim.
> Th'unwearied sun, from day to day,
> Does his Creator's powers display,
> And publishes to every land
> The work of an Almighty Hand.
>
> What though in solemn silence all
> Move round the dark terrestrial ball?
> What though no real voice nor sound
> Amid the radiant orbs be found?
> In reason's ear they all rejoice,
> And utter forth a glorious voice,
> Forever singing as they shine,
> *"The hand that made us is divine."* [90]

Always we stand in peril of either humanising God too much, so that his majesty is diminished in our eyes, or of exalting him so high that he loses sympathy. A balance must be achieved. It is here that a study of the divine attributes (such as we are now undertaking) can be helpful.

Many aspects of the divine nature could be called *communicable*, that is, they can in some measure be shared

---

[90] Joseph Addison; first published in The Spectator, London, England; 1712.

by humans. Indeed, some would say that *every* attribute is partially imparted to us who are made in the image and likeness of God. Others argue that the boundless perfection of God makes it impossible for any of his perfections to be conveyed to us. Perhaps a more reasonable approach would allow that some of the divine attributes are more communicable than others, and that at best we can share any of them only in a limited and sin-darkened measure.

Along with many that I have already mentioned, a commonly accepted list of communicable attributes would probably include the following –

- ***spirituality*** – which we express through worship and prayer
- ***intelligence*** – which we express through knowledge, wisdom, truth
- ***morality*** – which we express through goodness, grace, mercy, holiness, righteousness, justice, and the like.
- ***emotion*** – which we express through love, friendship, laughter, joy, kindness, anger, grief, and the like.

God is able to communicate these attributes to his servants in a generous measure, although always far short of the absolute perfection in which God himself possesses them.

Some have argued, however, that certain attributes of God are altogether *incommunicable* – they cannot be shared by any creature. Those *incommunicable attributes* of God are eternally true of him and have no relation to the creation. That is, whether or not the universe came into existence, those attributes of God would remain perfect for ever. They are those things that above all mark his incontestable Deity, his almighty sovereignty, his total self-sufficiency and entire self-existence. They are absolutely and uniquely divine and cannot be imparted to any creature.

Others say that all the attributes are divine, eternal, and in no way contingent upon the existence of a physical universe, and that all of them are in a greater or lesser measure communicable, especially to God's own children in Christ. It is a debate that seems unlikely to be resolved prior to the Second Advent!

Still, we may freely allow that some of the aspects of God's nature and being, and portions of each of his attributes, at least in their full perfection, are uniquely divine, shared by no other being in the entire universe. There is no harm, for our purposes here, in calling them *incommunicable*. What are the benefits of thinking about these incommunicable aspects of God?

THEY ENGENDER HUMBLE DEPENDENCE

There will always be an infinite gulf between humans and God. Scripture never suggests that we will ever become part of God, or be absorbed back into God. Indeed, the folly of trying to usurp that which belongs only to God is shown by the results of the Fall. Adam and Eve tried to commandeer divine prerogatives and were at once banished from the Garden (Ge 3:5, 23-24).

THEY ENGENDER AWE AND REVERENCE

> *Watch your step when you go to church. It is better to go there to learn than to make wild promises. Why brand yourself a fool who can't tell right from wrong? So think before you speak, and don't make vows that you won't honour. God is in heaven and you are on earth, so don't say any more than you have to ... But if you do make a promise to God, make*

> *sure that you keep it. God has no liking for people who say what they don't mean. Far better not to make any promise than having made one, fail to keep it. (Ec 5:1-7)*

THEY ENGENDER RESTFUL TRUST

The more one contemplates the grandeur and glory of the Lord God, the more one realises that he is too great to be hurried or anxious; he never runs, he walks! We have to do things by the exertion of energy, by the sweat of our brows; but God needs only to *speak*. One word, and it is done! He *says*, and it *is* !

Well, if those are some of the *values* of the incommunicable attributes of God, which of his attributes are in fact *incommunicable* ?

ATTRIBUTES OF SPLENDOUR

Among people who like to divide the attributes of God into communicable and incommunicable, there are generally said to be five *Incommunicable Attributes* of God –

- Omnipotence
- Omnipresence
- Omniscience
- Immutability
- Infinity

We can say of these attributes (as indeed is true of all that I have mentioned in these pages) that they are qualities of the entire Godhead, equally and fully; that they are eternal, and will never change; that they are inseparable from the very being and nature of God – they cannot ever diminish, nor be replaced, nor altered in any respect. They not only *belong* to

God, they *are* God, qualities that define who he is and what he does.

Let us begin with the first of them –

OMNIPOTENCE

To say that the Lord God is *omnipotent* means that he possesses infinite might, boundless strength, limitless ability, untrammelled power. This supernal potency is shown in three ways. It is –

KNOWN BY THE THINGS GOD <u>CAN</u> DO

What can he do? *"Anything he pleases!"* – whether in heaven or on earth (Ps 135:5-7). That is, God is limited only by his own choice and character; no boundary nor restraint can be placed upon his actions save those that are

- ***inherent in his nature*** as a non-corporeal and morally perfect spirit [91] – therefore he cannot sin, nor do anything unrighteous, for to do so would break his own commandment; nor can he lie, for that would violate his inner holiness; and so on.
- ***determined by his will*** (which nothing can finally or successfully thwart) – therefore he cannot either deny his promise nor act against it; neither can he ignore his own decrees, but is bound to do as he has said he will do, to keep faith with the entire creation and to obey the dictates of his own will.

---

(91) Hence, he cannot play tennis or play a violin, eat an orange or sleep on a bed, for such activities require a body; nor can he do anything that offends universal moral law.

- ***logically inconsistent*** – therefore he cannot design a square circle, nor create at the same time both an immovable object and an irresistible force, ⁽⁹²⁾ nor make a stone so heavy that he cannot lift it, ⁽⁹³⁾ nor do anything that violates reason or contradicts ordinary logic.

However, I acknowledge the need for caution in pre-determining what is "logical" and "reasonable" when talking about God. Certainly, the normal canons of sound thinking must govern the mind of God, as they do our minds, for we are made in his likeness, and God himself bids us to *"reason together"* with him (Is 1:18). Nonetheless the gulf between a finite and an infinite mind is immeasurable. So the Lord also says –

> *"My thoughts are not your thoughts, and my ways are not your ways," declares the Lord.*

---

(92) My father used to tease his children with this problem, "What happens when an irresistible force strikes an immovable object?" If we said that the object blew up, he would rejoin that it is immovable. If we said that the force was turned aside, he would insist that it was irresistible. He reduced us almost to tears of vexation! I was several years older before I realised that the problem was not physical but semantic – that is, if there is such a thing as an irresistible force, then there cannot be an immovable object; and vice versa. At least one of them has to be removed from the universe before the other can truly exist.

(93) The problem here, as my previous footnote suggests is semantic more than real. That is, it is a problem created more by the words used rather than by anything real. For all that, whatever one calls it, a square is square and cannot be round. Similarly, this question must always be irrational, "Can God make a stone so heavy that not even he can lift it?" Such a stone would have to be bigger than the universe, bigger than God himself. But by simplest definition, God is and must always be the biggest entity that exists or can even be imagined.

> *"Just as the heavens are higher than the earth,
> so my ways are higher than your ways, and
> my thoughts are higher than your thoughts."*
> *(Is 55:8-9)*

Hence, while I normally trust that sensible thinking will accord with the mind of God, it may not always be so. Jesus walked on water, hushed a storm with a word, rode an untamed donkey through a cheering crowd, and raised others and himself from the dead! None of that agrees too well with human logic, but it happened nonetheless!

KNOWN BY THE THINGS GOD <u>REFRAINS</u> FROM DOING

Martin Luther once said, "If I were God, and the world treated me as it treats him, I would kick the wretched thing to pieces!" (94) Instead, God sent his Son to die for a fallen race.

But Luther's words do suggest one element of divine omnipotence – to achieve his purpose the Lord God has no need of force. He may often seem to do nothing, yet does everything. At the moment, it may seem that heaven is impotent or uncaring; but the years pass, and suddenly, looking back, one can see how sure and firm was the Lord's guiding hand. And if it does not yet seem so, then wait longer. In time, either this side of the resurrection, or the other, you will echo the sacred writer and cry – *"Praise the Lord, for he has kept every promise, and given us everything that he promised!"* (1 Kg 8:56)

---

(94) If anyone can tell me the source of this saying, I would be grateful. It is quoted many times on the internet, but so far I have been unable to discover its origin.

Scripture in several places describes the remarkable way in which God, without seeming to do so, works irresistibly to achieve his ends. This is perhaps the greatest sign of God's omnipotence – his serene silence, his patient restraint (cp. Ma 3:6; Ps 78:38). He acts while not appearing to act; he works when there is no sign of his working.

In his omnipotence, God can do all that he wills, but he does not will all that he can do; his strength is shown not only by what he says, but by what he does not say; not only by what he does, but by what he does not do.

God does not act without motive, nor under necessity, except for what his own nature demands. Otherwise, he does only what he chooses. He acts only as he pleases. His purpose is set, and he will achieve it.

There is nothing aimless nor indecisive in the Lord. On the contrary there is a quality of *ruthlessness* in his will, for he will brook no diminution of his glorious design. No decision by a single man nor by the entire race of men can ever thwart even the least part of his will. Yet he does this without impinging upon our freedom of choice. He gives each of us liberty to say *"No!"* He is able to, and does, bring his plans to fruition serenely, invisibly, while refraining from overt imposition upon any of us. And he achieves this without doing any sort of violence to his own character of holiness and love.

I do not mean that God cannot intervene anywhere in the universe both violently and forcefully, nor that he will not do so. On the contrary, scripture itself tells us that one day Christ will come in awesome power, and all the holy angels with him, to rapture his church, to execute heaven's wrath upon a stubbornly rebellious world, and to inaugurate a new heaven and a new earth. But for now, the Lord God displays his relentless power by refraining from such dramatic displays, and by working usually unseen, unheard, and unfelt, yet just as surely accomplishing his purpose.

KNOWN BY THE THINGS GOD <u>CANNOT</u> DO

God cannot *deny* himself (2 Ti 2:13). Therefore, he cannot alter history; he cannot sin, die, falsify his own knowledge, betray his own purpose, break his own decrees, nor act contrary to his own character. He cannot put the used toothpaste back into its tube, nor the peel back onto an eaten apple. He cannot cause a grown man to shrink back to an infant and re-enter his mother's womb. He cannot make water dry, nor black white, nor the truth a lie. He cannot do anything that contravenes his spoken or written word. He cannot abandon integrity, truth, righteousness, or justice. He cannot act against his own being.

And perhaps above all, for us, he cannot, prior to the Day of Judgment, deny human free will.

In every circumstance, dealing with every person, and with angels, God can do only what is consistent with, or worthy of, himself and of his fixed decrees.

Think carefully about the limitation of divine power. He may be omnipotent, yet God cannot just do *anything*; he can do only what he *pleases*, and he pleases to do only what is *consistent* with his holiness and love.

Let me come back again to the child's question, "Can God make a rock so heavy he can't lift it?" To reply either "yes" or "no" defies logic; the question is simply absurd. Why? Because rocks exist only as created things, in conformity with a divine decree, limited by God's own definition of what is a rock, and subject to his physical laws. So a rock comprising all the matter in the universe would no longer be a *"rock"*, it would be something else altogether. Therefore not even God can make a *"rock"* so big, for this would require him to do something his own decrees bind him not to do.

Perhaps strangely, yet very important for us humans, in scripture the omnipotence of God is not so much measured by the physical universe, as by three special events –

THE EXODUS

- see *Psalm 77:11-20; 106:8-12*; this was the measure, the standard example, of divine power during the entire OT period. The ancient Israelites could envision no mightier demonstration of divine omnipotence.

THE RESURRECTION

- Christ's conquest of death opened a new standard of limitless power (Ep 1:19-20; 1 Pe 1:13).

THE RAPTURE

- the final result of the exodus, and of Christ's resurrection, will be the rapture of the church, which Paul says will require God to *"transform our lowly body to be like his glorious body, by the power that enables him even to subject all things to himself"*. (Ph 3:20-21).

Note how each of those special examples show that we should look for the greatest display of divine power, not in the natural world, but in the deliverance God achieves for his people.

Finally, God's omnipotence is expressed through his spoken *word* (Ge 1:1-3; Ro 4:17; He 1:3; 11:3). This omnipotence now resides in us (Ep 1:19-20), not *directly* but *indirectly* through our union with Christ, and can be released by his word, when that word is boldly spoken in faith.

FIFTEEN

EVERYWHERE

> Where can I go to escape from your Spirit?
> *How can I hide from your sight?*
> *If I fly far into space, you will be there.*
> *If I plunge into the deepest abyss, you will find me.*
> *If I had the wings of the morning and flew far to the east,*
> *Or chased the ocean's horizon to the uttermost west,*
> *Still your hand would be there to lead me,*
> *And I would be upheld by your strong arm.*
> *Suppose I find a dark place to hide until day turns to night?*
> *You will find me in a moment, for daylight and darkness are the same to you.*
> *You see me in the darkest night as if it were the brightest day!* (95)

Said one boy to another, "Is God in my pocket?"

"Of course he is!"

"No he isn't. – I haven't got a pocket!"

Pocket or not, God is still everywhere, hence it is impossible to escape from his presence. Scholars call this the doctrine of God's **omnipresence** – that is, he is everywhere present at the same time (see Ps 139:7-10; Pr 15:3; Je 23:23-24; Mt 28:20). This "presence" gives to the doctrine a unique aspect – unlike the other major attributes of God, this one is true only in regard to the physical creation, what we call the "time-space continuum", for apart from the creation he

---

(95) Psalm 139:7-12, paraphrased.

would be called *"Infinite"* rather than *"Omnipresent"*. And even "infinite" is not a good term, for it still conveys an idea of space. Perhaps "without any dimensions" would be better, but I'll come to the idea of "infinity" later. In the end, of course, no human words can correctly describe a God who vastly transcends the limitations that are inherent in any language.

When Elijah challenged the prophets of Baal to persuade their god to send fire from heaven, and they failed, he mocked them –

> *Why don't you shout louder? What kind of god is he? Perhaps he's gone aside to meditate, or maybe outside to relieve himself? He might be overseas and can't hear you. Or perhaps he's asleep and you have to wake him up!* (1 Kg 18:27)

The prophet meant that any god who was truly God would not be off somewhere else, but would necessarily be immanent to his creation, impossible to evade. So this attribute of omnipresence is essential for the very concept of deity. It is a divine attribute. It is not, and never can be, the possession of any creature, not even of the highest archangel, and assuredly not of Satan. Like every other creature, the devil has to *"walk to and fro"* (Jb 1:7), and even the chief archangel is bounded by space. The Lord God and he alone cannot "travel", for he is already everywhere it is possible to be.

This is one of the reasons why scripture forbids the erection of any idol, for how can the limitless God be depicted within the boundaries of a tangible form?

THREE OTHER ASPECTS OF GOD'S OMNIPRESENCE

John Wesley (1703-1791) once preached on the omnipresence of God, and began his sermon thus –

> Can there be in the whole compass of nature a more sublime subject? Can there be any more worthy the consideration of every rational creature? Is there any more necessary to be considered, and to be understood, so far as our poor faculties will admit? How many excellent purposes may it answer! What deep instruction may it convey to all the children of men! And more directly to the children of God. (96)

Three of those important aspects of omnipresence are –

GOD IS FULLY AND EQUALLY PRESENT EVERYWHERE

God is not diffused through space. He is not like the air of our planet, nor the ether of the wider universe, as if a bit of him were here, and a bit somewhere else. Rather, the entire creation is filled with God, and all of God fills each part of the creation. Martin Luther rightly protested against the crude idea that God is omnipresent only in the sense that he is the biggest thing in the universe, and is spread out across the universe –

> (That) is not our language. On the contrary, we deny that God is such an extended, long, broad, thick, high, low Being. We rather contend that

---

(96) *Number 111*, from the 1872 edition of <u>Wesley's Sermons</u>. Preached in Portsmouth, August 12, 1788.

> God is a supernatural, unfathomable Being, who at one and the same time is in every little kernel of grain and also in and above and outside all creatures. . . . Nothing is so small, God is still smaller; nothing is so large, God is still larger; nothing is so short, God is still shorter; nothing is so long, God is still longer; nothing is so wide, God is still wider; nothing is so narrow, God is still narrower; etc. In a word, God is an inexpressible Being, above and beyond everything that may be said or thought. (97)

So the whole of God is present in every part of the universe. The Lord is not *partly* with me, but with me in his *entirety*. All of God is in me, over me, under me, around me, with me, wherever I am, whatever I am doing.

GOD CANNOT WITHDRAW HIMSELF

God cannot withdraw himself from any part of the universe: *"in him we live and move and have our being"* (Ac 17:28). It is impossible to conceive of the absence of God. Even in hell he will be as present as he is in heaven, albeit in a different relationship, one of judgment rather than blessing. Were the Lord to withdraw himself from any part of the universe, even momentarily, it would cease to function, indeed, it would simply cease to *be*, for, as scripture says, *"he upholds everything by the word of his power"* (He 1:3).

How this omnipresence can be, we cannot tell. Even the psalmist, when he considered how God was equally with him and with all other creatures, was obliged to cry, *"Such*

---

(97)   E. M. Plass; op. cit., Vol. 2, pg. 543.

knowledge is too wonderful for me; it is high; I cannot attain it!" (Ps 139:6, ESV)

Note however, that God's omnipresence does not prevent him from destroying the material world or any part of his creation. Such an action would be a removal of the creature not of God himself. Thus the present heavens and earth are destined to dissolve away and to be replaced by new heavens and a new earth, filled with righteousness –

> *God spoke of his Son and said, "In the beginning Lord, you are the one who laid the foundations of the earth and created the heavens with your own hand. And when they all disappear, you will remain. They will wear out like old clothes; they will go out of date, but you will stay the same. Like a worn-out coat they will be thrown away and changed for something new, but you will never change and your life will never end. (He 1:10-12; and see also 2 Pe 3:11-13)*

What about biblical expressions that do indicate a divine departure? We should read them as describing, not the *removal* of God, but either as a change of *relationship* or as a *veiling* of awareness. That is, God's relationship with any part of his creation may change from one of pleasure to one of anger, from blessing to judgment, from upholding to casting down. Or, any of his creatures may vary in their awareness of God, from complete ignorance, to indifference, to rebellion, to unassailable love.

TRANSCENDENT AND IMMANENT

Omnipresence means that God, despite being gloriously transcendent is also intensely immanent –

> *"I am a God who is near. I am also a God who is far away," declares the Lord. "No one can hide so that I can't see him," declares the Lord. "I fill heaven and earth!" declares the Lord. (Je 23:23-24, GW)*

He is constantly at work in the world (Jn 5:17), whether on a cosmic or microscopic scale, to achieve his purpose for creation. Especially, he is actively involved in the affairs of his own people, to ensure their salvation, and to carry them safely from earth to glory –

> *For thus says the One who is high and lifted up, who inhabits eternity, whose name is Holy: "I dwell in the high and holy place, and also with him who is of a contrite and lowly spirit, to revive the spirit of the lowly, and to revive the heart of the contrite." (Is 57:15, ESV)*

God neither will nor can abandon those who trust him, but gives an unequivocal promise to be with them always, intimately and totally (He 13:5; De 31:6-8; Is 41:10).

PRACTICAL APPLICATION

Earlier in the *Psalm* that heads this meditation, the psalmist cries –

> *My Lord, you have looked deep into my heart and you know all about me. You know when I sit down and when I stand up. From heaven you read my mind and know all my thoughts. You watch me when I go out, and when I come home again. I have no secrets with you. Even before I speak a word you know what I am about to say. You surround me on every side,*

> *and your strong arm holds me up and protects me. (139:1-5)*

If those words are true (and who can doubt them?), then they demand of us, as John Wesley said, a certain response –

> Seeing you are continually under the eye of your Captain, how zealous and active should you be to "fight the good fight of faith, and lay hold on eternal life"; "to endure hardship, as good soldiers of Jesus Christ;" to use all diligence, to "war a good warfare", and to do whatever is acceptable in his sight! How studious should you be to approve all your ways to his all-seeing eyes; that he may say to your hearts, what he will proclaim aloud in the great assembly of men and angels, "Well done, good and faithful servants!"
>
> In order to attain these glorious ends, spare no pains to preserve always a deep, a continual, a lively, and a joyful sense of his gracious presence. Never forget his comprehensive word to the great father of the faithful: *"I am the Almighty* (rather, the All-sufficient) *God; walk before me, and be thou perfect!"* Cheerfully expect that he, before whom you stand, will ever guide you with his eye, will support you by his guardian hand, will keep you from all evil, and *"when you have suffered a while, will make you perfect, will establish, strengthen, and settle you"*; and then *"preserve you unblameable, unto the coming of our Lord Jesus Christ!"* (98)

---

(98)   Op. cit. closing paragraphs.

SIXTEEN

PRESCIENCE

> God, who omniscient art,
> Could we from thee depart,
> Hide aught from thee,
> Thou, Lord, would search it out,
> Know all our sin and doubt,
> Searching within, without,
> Our secrets see. [99]

Cicero, the famous Roman orator and statesman, who was foully executed by the command of Octavian (who became Augustus Caesar), once wrote a treatise "On Divination". He said, in part –

> Can there be a just presentiment of those things which do not admit of any rational conjecture to explain why they will happen? For what do we mean when we say a thing happens by chance, or fortune, or hazard, or accident, but that something has happened or taken place which might never have happened or taken place at all, or which might have happened or taken place in a different manner? Now how can that be fairly foreseen or predicted which thus takes place by chance, and the mere caprice of fortune?

---

(99)   A paraphrase of Psalm 44, author unknown.

> How can it be foreseen that anything will happen which has neither any assignable cause, nor any mark, to show why it will happen? ...
>
> If these events, and others of the same kind, happen by any kind of necessity, then what is there that we can suppose to be brought about by chance or fortune? For nothing is so opposite to regularity and reason as this same fortune; *so that it seems to me that God himself cannot foreknow absolutely those things which are to happen by chance and fortune.* For if he knows it, then it will certainly happen; and if it will certainly happen, there is no chance in the matter. But there is chance; therefore there is no such thing as a presentiment of the future. (100)

Thus Cicero long ago presented the chief problem that confronts those who claim that God *does* have and *must* have detailed knowledge of all that is yet to happen. If God *does* possess total prescience, how can there be any room left for freedom of choice, or for the future to be changed? The conclusion seems inescapable – if God infallibly knows everything that will happen in the future, then no human being can do anything to influence or change the future.

Yet if God does *not* possess such foreknowledge, how can we face tomorrow with joyful confidence? Does not much of our confidence in the Father's providence depend upon a sense that he knows all, that to him the path ahead is not obscure but plainly seen?

---

(100) Marcus Tullus Cicero (106-43 B.C.), De Divinatione, from 2:5-9. The italics are mine.

ARE WE WALKING INTO DARKNESS?

The pages that follow may be the most sensitive of all that I have ever written. I have often before marched boldly into mine-strewn fields, never doubting that I could pick a safe path. But this paddock is packed with perils! Anyone who raises questions about the extent of divine **_foreknowledge_** must expect to be assaulted on every side by a barrage of fiery darts!

Still, as always when a matter is doubtful, I will try to be fair to differing viewpoints and in the end allow my readers to make up their own minds about what they should believe. In the meantime, for those who may soon start bristling like the proverbial hedgehog, let me echo the words of Oliver Cromwell (1599-1658), who in a letter to the crusty General Assembly of the Church of Scotland (August 3rd, 1650) pleaded, "I beseech you, in the bowels of Christ, think it possible that you may be mistaken!"

Or if you mislike Cromwell, try Omar Khayyam (c. 1048- c. 1122), Persian poet, mathematician, and astronomer, who wrote the following quatrain about doctrinal squabbles (which are as endemic in Islam as they are in Christendom) –

> One lot cogitates on the way of religion;
> Another ponders on the path of mystical certainty;
> But I fear one day the cry will go up –
> "Oh you fools, neither this nor that is the way!" [101]

Or in the words of Edward Fitzgerald's translation of another of the Persian sage's quatrains –

---

(101) The Ruba'iyat of Omar Khayyam, tr. by Peter Avery and John-Heath-Stubbs; Penguin Classics, 1983; Quatrain 220.

> Myself when young did eagerly frequent
> Doctor and Saint, and heard great argument
> About it and about; but evermore
> Came out by the same door as in I went. (102)

In other words, be wary whenever someone claims to be a proclaimer of infallible dogma! Across the entire span of church history no denominational statement of faith nor any church creed has ever been wholly free of error. You may at once retort, "That sentence is surely dogmatic enough!" True, but it has the benefit of visible proof in the continuing quarrels that divide the church into so many diverse groups. It is simply absurd when any of them claim to be the sole guardians of truth. They are all wrong to some degree. (103)

Since, then, any of us may be mistaken at some time or other, we should hold gracious charity toward each other's foibles. Therefore, I ask you to accept that some of the ideas that I think are false may in the end prove to be true, while some that you now think are true may prove to be false. Jesus alone can say, *"I am the Truth!"*

SOMETHING WE CAN ALL AGREE ON

We are thinking here about what God <u>knows</u>, and the doctrine that is called **omniscience**, or the possession of *all-knowledge*. It is one of the most difficult of the attributes of God to explain, which has not deterred countless divines

---

(102) *Quatrain Number 30* in the Fitzgerald translation.

(103) I do not exclude myself from that admission of error. I shudder sometimes when I wonder how many of my own opinions and beliefs will be shown to be wrong on the Day of Judgment. I can only hope they will not be too numerous, but I shall be very surprised if there are none!

from trying to do so, some with more success than others. Whether the following pages will prove to be better or worse than their efforts, you will have to determine for yourself.

We can at least agree that **_whatever is knowable, God knows_**. Whether in the past, present, or future, if a piece of knowledge exists, then it is fully known to God.

Let us also agree that *if something is not knowable*, then not even God can know it, for that would be a contradiction of his own decrees. To enquire if God can know the unknowable is logically akin to the child's question, "Did God make himself?" or, "Can God make a circle square?" To answer either yes or no is to involve oneself in absurdity, because the very word "God" means "the one who is self-existent" and "the one who cannot contravene himself".

So the question about whether or not the Lord God has complete knowledge of the future is not one about *omniscience* (for God does indeed know everything that can be known); rather, it is an enquiry about the extent to which the *future* is knowable. If the future is knowable, <u>then God knows it</u>. If the future is not knowable, <u>then God does not know it</u>.

Let us begin then by looking at

TWO CONFLICTING OPINIONS ON OMNISCIENCE

There is, first, the <u>*orthodox*</u> view, which holds that God knows everything that ever has happened, is happening, and ever will happen.

Then there is, second, the <u>*openness*</u> view, which holds that God has only a partial knowledge of the future.

Let me say at once that I am uneasy with *both* views, because neither of them seems to have any absolute biblical warrant, and also because intuition and logic lead me to view both of them with a degree of suspicion. In other words, I find it difficult to accept either that

- God has *absolute* innate prescience (knowledge of the future); or that
- God has *no* innate prescience.

Both views seem to me to treat scripture less than honestly. They savour too much of an unbiblical dogmatism, and they create either a measure of discomfort or a degree of irrationality.

WHAT THEN CAN WE AFFIRM?

We can at least affirm this –

- with respect to the **_past_** – God knows it absolutely, for nothing has ever been hidden or can be hidden from his all-seeing eye;
- with respect to the **_present_** – God knows this too, absolutely, for he is totally aware of every thought, word, or action that is now occurring.

But what about the **_future_** ? To what degree is the future knowable? If it **is** knowable in its entirety, then God knows it. But if the future is **not** knowable, then not even God knows it, for it is illogical to say that something unknowable is yet known.

So once again, the real question is not, *"Does God know the future?"* but *"Is the future knowable?"* For if it is knowable, then God knows it; but if it is not knowable, then God does not know it.

An associated question also arises: if the future *is* knowable, then to what extent? Is it knowable *in full*, or only *in part* ?

But then this question comes down to one that is even more fundamental, namely, *what is the future?* Does the future actually *exist* ? If it does exist, then how *can* it exist, since it has not yet happened? Does it exist only in the foreknowledge of God? But then, how can even God foreknow something that has not yet happened, and that may not happen, unless he himself has decreed it? (104)

Perhaps God has decreed the future, in its entirety? If so, what effect would such a decree have upon human freedom of choice? Or, if the future is open, what effect would this have upon divine sovereignty? Or, if the future is open yet fixed in the knowledge of God, how would that affect both people and God?

Nonetheless, if the future does exist, then God knows it; if it does not exist, then God does not know it, for yet again, not even God can know the unknowable.

What follows is an attempt to make sense out of these questions, depending first on scripture, then on whatever other evidence seems useful.

But first, may I draw your attention again to the first *Addendum* at the end of this book? ("Some Insuperable Hurdles"). It reminds us that the very greatest apostles, the finest thinkers, the most brilliant scholars, are all stuck with the fact that we are *at best* people *"looking through a dark glass"*, whose knowledge can never in this life be more than partial (1 Co 13:9,12). So it behoves us to be wary of dogmatism. Our noblest truths are seldom better than approximations; and nowhere is that more so than when we endeavour to encompass an infinite God within the boundaries of finite language. So let us maintain grace and

---

(104) See meditation *Twenty-Two* below, on the nature of time.

humility as we strive to glimpse some fresh facets of the beauty and wonder of our glorious Lord.

SEVENTEEN

FOREKNOWLEDGE

> Come, O thou Prophet of the Lord,
> Thou great interpreter divine,
> Explain thine own transmitted word,
> To teach and to inspire is thine;
> Thou only canst thyself reveal,
> Open the book and loose the seal!
> – Charles Wesley

Christian theology, following Augustine (circa 400 A.D.), has usually insisted that God not only *has* but *must* have complete and detailed knowledge of everything *past*, *present*, and *future*. Thus Augustine wrote –

> *"God saw that it was good"* (Ge 1:31). This statement, applied to all his works, can only signify the approval of work done with the true artist's skill, which here is the Wisdom of God. It is not that God discovered that it was good, after it had been made. Far from it. Not one of those works would have been done, if he had not known it beforehand. It could not have come into being if he had not seen it already; and so when he "sees that it is good" he is not discovering that fact, but communicating it. . . . (The) finished work met with the artist's approval, as he had before approved it as something for his art to make. . . .
>
> It is not with God as it with us. He does not look ahead to the future, look directly at the present, look back to the past. He sees in some

> other manner, utterly remote from anything we experience or could imagine. He does not see things by turning his attention from one thing to another. He sees all without any kind of change. Things which happen under the condition of time, are in the future, not yet in being, or in the present, already existing, or in the past, no longer in being. But God comprehends all these in a stable and eternal present. . . .
>
> Nor does his attention pass from one thought to another; all things which he knows are present at the same time to his incorporeal vision. He knows events in time without any temporal knowledge, just as he moves events in time, without any temporal motions in himself. (105)

There is, of course, no argument about God's perfect knowledge of all that lies in the *past* and in the *present*; the quarrel is about how much of the *future* is known to God

Thus some (following Aristotle rather than Augustine, and agreeing with Cicero) have argued that for humans to have true freedom of choice we must assert that

- while God must have perfect knowledge of all that *has* happened or *is* happening, he can do no more than conjecture the shape of the future, except that
- he is fully aware of every single *possibility* inherent in the future; that is, he knows the possible outcome of

---

(105) The City of God, Book XI, Ch. 21; tr. by Henry Bettenson; ed. by David Knowles; Penguin Books, London, 1972.

every present action; he knows the total number of possible futures; and he

- certainly knows what he himself has chosen or ordained shall happen, for his decrees cannot be changed by time or circumstance; [106]
- but since all other choices can be, and often are changed, therefore
- the future must be contingent upon both human and divine choices and cannot be fully known until those choices have actually been made. [107]

Consider, for example, the implicit invitation in the *Lord's Prayer* to become a partner with God in giving final shape to the future –

> *"May your Kingdom come, and may your will be done on earth, just as it is in heaven."*

Those words strongly imply that at least in some measure the dawning of the kingdom of God is dependent upon the prayers of the church. If our prayers can have no influence

---

(106) God is powerful enough, and wise enough, to make whatever decree he pleases about the future, without impinging upon human freedom of choice. As Jesus himself said, when the people were rebuked by some Jewish leaders for acclaiming him as King, "If these people do not speak, then the very stones will shout aloud instead!" (Lu 19:40; and cp. Mt 3). In other words, whatever individual people may choose to do, the will of God cannot be thwarted.

(107) Those who hold to the orthodox view would reply that God's future choices have already been made, and cannot be changed, for it is impossible that the infinite, perfect, and almighty God could ever be subject to any kind of alteration. But that creates an image of a drearily static deity, and gives little credit to scores of biblical references that describe the Lord as responding spontaneously to shifting circumstances on earth.

upon the coming of that wonderful day, why pray? It is difficult to avoid the conclusion that the time of its coming is not yet fixed, that there is a degree of openness about the future.

Note also that there is nothing in the present state of affairs which necessarily predetermines for all events their final outcome. Some outcomes are certain; some are probable; some are only possible; and some are as yet quite unknown. Yet if God already does know the final outcome of everything, surely that leaves us fixed into a kind of stasis from which all spontaneous ebb and flow has been removed?

Further, to say that God has a perfect knowledge of the future choices of morally free agents seems to be an assertion that something can be known even though it does not yet exist and there are no other grounds for knowing it – which on the face of it is an absurdity. Yet, as you will see just below, there is biblical evidence for the idea that God *does* know everything that will happen – every thought, word, action, circumstance, or occurrence that will ever occur, not only on earth, but throughout the entire creation.

Which of those alternative views is correct? Consider the following –

COMMON BIBLICAL EVIDENCE

> God from all eternity, did, by the most wise and holy counsel of his own will, freely, and unchangeably ordain whatsoever comes to pass; yet so, as thereby neither is God the author of sin, nor is violence offered to the will of the creatures; nor is the liberty or contingency of second causes taken away, but rather established.

> Although God knows whatsoever may or can come to pass upon all supposed conditions; yet has he not decreed anything because he foresaw it as future, or as that which would come to pass upon such conditions. (108)

The worthy scholars who composed that confession were untroubled by doubts! They declare unequivocally that God has decreed the future in its entirety, and has done so without first checking on what anyone on earth was doing. They also declare that notwithstanding the divine decree, we creatures are still in full possession of freedom of choice, and nor can God be blamed for anything that happens in the future, even though he decreed it. Nor did the learned divines make any attempt to reconcile those apparent contradictions.

Well, I have to say that that is all a bit too subtle for me, and smacks more of dogma than it does of scripture.

Still, they do not lack a good measure of biblical support. The passages usually quoted to support that classical idea that God has a perfect knowledge of everything past, present, and future would include the following – Nu 23:19; 1 Sa 2:3; 15:29; 23:9-13; Jb 12:13; Ps 94:9; 139:4; 147:4; Is 29:15; 40:27,28; 41:21-22; 42:9; 44:23-28; 46:9-10; Je 32:6-9; 38:17-23; 42:9-22; Da 2:28; Zc 11:12; Ma 3:6; Mt 11:21-23; 24:36; 26:18 (Mk 14:13-16; Lu 22:10-13); Mt 26:23-25; 27:9; Jn 18:4 (*"Jesus, knowing all that was about to happen to him . . ."*); Ac 2:23; 3:18; 15:17-18; Ro 8:29; 11:2; He 4:13; Ja 1:17; 1 Pe 1:2; 1 Jn 3:20; etc.

We may particularly note Jesus' predictions about his arrest, trial, crucifixion, resurrection, and ascension. He foretold

---

(108)   Westminster Confession of Faith 3:1-2 (written in 1647).

Peter's betrayal; he predicted the persecution of his church; and of course, in what is called the *Olivet Discourse*, he spoke many oracles about the future (Mt 24, Mk 13, Lu 21). Or think about Jesus' affirmation, *"Your Father knows what you need before you ask him!"* (Mt 6:8)

Some have seen another assertion of divine prescience in the anonymous words, "But the ungodly were assailed to the end by pitiless anger, *for God knew in advance even their future actions*" (Wis 19:1). That passage may indeed suggest divine foreknowledge, but others think it refers more to God's own decree, as a later verse shows –

> For the fate they deserved drew them on to this end, and made them forget what had happened, in order that they might fill up the punishment that their torments still lacked. (vs. 4, NRSV)

Nonetheless, in the orthodox view it is claimed –

> (God) knows beforehand what Abraham will do, and what will happen to him; he knows beforehand that Pharaoh's heart will be hardened, and that Moses will deliver Israel (Ge 15:13 ff.; Ex 3:19; 7:4; 11:1 ff.).

> Nothing future is hidden from Yahweh (Is 41:22 ff.; 42:9; 43:9-13; 44:6-8; 46:10; Da 2:22; Am 3:7), and this foreknowledge embraces the entire course of man's life (Ps 31:15); 39:5; 139:4-6; 139:16; Jb 14:5). These passages from Isaiah show that it is from the occurrence of events in accordance with Yahweh's prediction that the Prophet will prove his foreknowledge; and that in contrast with the worshippers of idols which are taken by surprise, Israel is warned of the future by the omniscient Yahweh.

> In the New Testament, foreknowledge in the sense of prescience is ascribed to God. Jesus asserts a foreknowledge by God of that which is hidden from the Son (Mk 13:32), and James asserts that all God's works are foreknown by him (Ac 15:18). Moreover, the many references in the New Testament to the fulfilment of prophecy all imply that the New Testament writers ascribed foreknowledge, in this sense of foresight, to God. (109)

Or again, on *2 Samuel 23:9-13* Don Stewart writes –

> Here we find a great example of God knowing all future possibilities. David and his men were in the city of Keilah. David asked the Lord what would happen if Saul came to Keilah. Would the men of Keilah deliver David and his men over to his enemy King Saul? The Lord answered with a yes. If Saul came to destroy Keilah, the men of that city would not fight. They would hand over David and his men to Saul. This is the fate that awaited David if Saul came to Keilah. Once David had that knowledge, he and his men escaped, preventing his being taken captive by Saul.
>
> God, therefore told David about a potential event in the future that never happened. God's knowledge extends not only to actual events that will occur, but every possible event that could occur. This gives further testimony to the omniscience of God. God not only knows what actually will happen, he also knows what

---

(109) International Standard Bible Encyclopedia, in. loc.

> potentially would have happened had David remained. (110)

Or again, Marvin Padgett writes –

> Is God in total control over his creation? Can he know the future? Does he have a pre-determined plan of all things that come to pass or is he ... waiting to see what happens and then come to the rescue. The Bible gives a clear response. For example, *Isaiah 40-48* assert that the reason Israel may safely believe in God is because he not only knows the future exhaustively, but controls the future exhaustively. (111) (In particular, see *Isaiah 41:21-24.)*

I grew up believing that classical view, and held to it for the first decade or so of my ministry. But then someone drew my attention to a phrase in the *Lord's Prayer* – *"Thy kingdom come, thy will be done, in earth as it is in heaven"* (Mt 6:10; Lu 11:2; KJV) Now, as I have already suggested, if that request has any meaning, then our prayers can hasten the coming of the Kingdom of God, which implies that the future must be at least to some degree *open*. We appear to be invited into partnership with God in shaping the future. I was so struck by this that I began to investigate the matter further, and found that

- despite the claims made by orthodox scholars, many, if not all the references cited above, and others like

---

(110)   From an online article at
        http://www.blueletterbible.org/faq/nbi/363.html.

(111)   From an online article at
        http://www.wrfnet.org/articles/printarticle.asp?ID=726.

them, may be given a more localised or narrower reading; based either upon some divine decree, or merely upon knowledge of contemporary events, or upon a particular way of using scripture

- for example, the oracle cited in *Matthew 27:9* is not actually a prophecy about future events – rather (as in other NT citations from the OT) it is used to demonstrate the principle that past events show a pattern that may often be repeated in both divine and human affairs
- none of the cited references state unequivocally that God possesses exhaustive knowledge of every future thought, decision, choice, and event, throughout the entire universe.

Thus, such passages as *Isaiah 41:21-24; 46:9-10; 48:3-5*, may be construed, not as a claim by Yahweh that he knows all the future, but rather as an assertion that he has power to shape future events in any way he pleases (in contrast with ineffectual pagan idols).

FURTHER EVIDENCE

Why then have scholars given the scriptures a broader meaning than their wording actually requires? I suppose, because of other considerations, such as these –

> If God cannot foreknow free human acts, then *"the Lamb that hath been slain from the foundation of the world"* (Re 13:8) was only a sacrifice to be offered in case Adam should fall, God not knowing whether he would or not, and in case Judas should betray Christ, God not knowing whether he would or not. Indeed, since the course of nature is changed by man's will when he burns towns and fells forests, God

> cannot on this theory predict even the course of nature. All prophecy is therefore a protest against (the view that God has only a limited knowledge of the future). (112)

That is to say, scripture shows that God does have foreknowledge of at least some thoroughly contingent events (1 Sa 23:10-13; 2 Kg 13:19; Ps 81:14,15; Is 48:18; Je 1:4-5; 38:17-20; etc.) (113) Hence Sirach wrote (circa B.C. 200) –

> The eyes of the Lord are ten thousand times brighter than the sun, observing every step that men and women take and searching out every secret place. Long before everything was created it was all known to God, and since their completion he continues to know everything. . . From the beginning to the end of time God can see everything, nothing is too marvellous for him nor beyond his understanding. . . God measures the abyss and the human heart, he searches out their most hidden secrets. Can anything remain unknown to the Lord God? Whatever is knowable, he knows! Before the beginning of all things he knows their end. He reveals what has been and what will be, and lays bare everything that tries to remain hidden. Not even a single thought can escape his notice, and not a word escapes his ear. (23:19-20; 39:20; 42:18-20)

---

(112) A. H. Strong, <u>Systematic Theology</u>; Pickering & Inglis Ltd, London, 1958; pg. 285.

(113) Louis Berkhof, <u>Systematic Theology</u>; Banner of Truth Trust, Grand Rapids, 1976; pg. 67.

Thus the ancient rabbi expressed his confidence in divine omniscience, a confidence that was echoed by the unknown author of the story of *Susanna*, who cried –

> Everlasting God, you know every secret, and you foresee every event! (vs. 42)

But another passage from the *Apocrypha* refers God's knowledge of the future to his own decrees. In it, Judith recounts one of the miracles that God did in the past to rescue his people, and then she declares –

> All that happened then, and all that happened before and after, was your work. What is now and what is yet to be, you have planned; and what you have planned has come to pass. The things you have foreordained present themselves and say, "We are here." All your ways are prepared beforehand; your judgment rests on foreknowledge. (Judith 9:5-6, REB). [114]

So it may be true to say that all the scriptures cited can be explained in lesser terms [115] than supposing that God knows

---

(114)   The passage no doubt reflects the deep fatalism of ancient Israel. Indeed, such fatalism (everything that happens has been pre-determined by God), is one way of solving the problem of divine foreknowledge. "Of course God knows everything about the future, for has he not decreed it?" But this sits ill with Christian concepts of freedom of choice and personal responsibility for one's actions. Nonetheless, the passage certainly holds that whatever God <u>has</u> decreed will infallibly come to pass.

(115)   Such as a divine decree, or God's perfect knowledge of the human heart and of existing events, trends, pressures, and the like (see below, under "What God does know"). Note also, that God is always able to over-ride human freedom of choice, not by ... *continued on next page* ....

the future as omnisciently as he knows the past and the present.

Further, there are many scriptures that seem to require us to infer an unknowable future, as we shall see later. Perhaps unhappily for us, the Bible is somewhat ambiguous on the subject, providing texts that both sides can use to support their case. (116) One is tempted to abandon the question! Yet we must try to arrive at some definition, because several important aspects of Christian life are affected by what one believes about divine foreknowledge –

- **_Prayer_** – is there any point in praying, if God already knows both what we will ask and what his answer will be? Surely this would reduce prayer to mere ritual, much as it is in Islam? (117)
- **_Suffering_** – if God knows in detail what will happen, how does this affect our sense of his justice, and why does he not act soon enough to steer us away from threatening peril?

---

	stifling it, but by so arranging events that his purpose is fulfilled whatever men and women may choose. As the old gospel song says, when God wanted the Canaanites to run away from the army of Israel, "he just made them willing to go!" He sent upon them a horde of angry hornets. It was their choice to run; but the Lord made certain that they had no other choice!
(116)	You can easily prove the truth of this by going online and searching out "foreknowledge". You will soon learn that scores of scholars around the world are furiously arguing the case on one side or the other. When so many experts disagree, sometimes with much passion, it behoves ordinary mortals to tread cautiously!
(117)	In Islam, prayer is not a request for something to change, or for God to do something, but rather an act of worshipful submission to the inscrutable and irresistible will of Allah.

- ***Evangelism*** – does God already know who will or will not be saved, and what effect should this have on our missionary mandate?
- ***The Future*** – why should we bother planning for it if God knows today all that will happen tomorrow?
- ***Providence*** – what measure of control does God exercise over events today to compel them to conform to the future already fixed in his knowledge? And, as Cicero asked, how can there be any such thing as "chance" or "accident" if the future is already fixed in the knowledge of God? Yet we sense that an accident is exactly that – an unplanned and unfortunate event that results in damage or an injury (Encarta). We sense, too, that many things, like winning a lottery, do happen by chance, without plan or purpose. It is hard to deny the reality of that sense, yet how can it be held in the face of a foreknown future?

The classical view may seem appealing (at least in certain circumstances), but does it fit the broad affirmations of scripture? Does it depend only upon certain proof texts? Does it successfully fit the over-all picture that scripture gives of God?

There is in one sense a great comfort to be found in the idea that God fully knows and fully controls every future happening, while there is something scary about supposing that God's knowledge of the future is limited. Yet there is also something suffocating about the idea of total prescience. A fully known future seems to be a wholly fixed future, which robs me of the freedom to change my mind. So let us look then at an alternative, that is, the idea of *openness*.

EIGHTEEN

OPENNESS

> Our times are in Thy hands;
> Father, we wish them there!
> Our life, our souls, our all we leave,
> Entirely to Thy care.
> Our times are in Thy hand,
> Whatever they may be;
> Pleasing or painful, dark or bright,
> As best may seem to Thee. (118)

Whatever **dogma** people may *believe* about the extent of God's foreknowledge, we all commonly **behave** as if the future were not yet fixed, as if our prayers can indeed change things, or even that God can be persuaded to change his mind. We enjoy a daily relationship with God that rests upon an assumption that God is responding to us moment by moment, without bias from what we may do or be in the future. That is, we *behave* as if the Lord does *not* know what we will do tomorrow, or at least is not influenced by it. We behave as if what we are doing now *does* have an affect upon God, and requires a response from God, and that the Lord has not already planned that response on the basis of some prior knowledge of every thought, word, or deed.

So it seems inescapable that all Christians who have real fellowship with the Father, do so upon the assumption of –

---

(118) William Lloyd (1627-1717), <u>Our Times are in Thy Hand</u>, st. 1 & 2; inspired by *Psalm 31:15*.

AN OPEN RELATIONSHIP

We cannot doubt that our relationship with God is immediate, dynamic, responsive, and free. Yet I find it difficult to imagine how such a relationship can be possible if the Lord already knows everything I will say or do. At least on the part of God, such prior knowledge would seem to remove all spontaneity from the relationship and render it static and dull. Yet I cannot help but believe that the Father finds as much delight in communing with me as I do with him, and that much of this delight arises from the joy of discovery, of surprise, of ever-renewing freshness – which must all vanish in the presence of an absolute foreknowledge of all things.

Likewise, can I have any genuine dialogue with God if I believe that nothing I say can surprise or even interest him, since every word of our conversation has been known to him from the beginning of time?

AN OPEN RESPONSE

Think about those places where the behaviour of people arouses God's **_anger_**. This seems to presuppose that the Lord did not anticipate their misdeeds – or at least that he had no prior detailed knowledge of them. Had he been fully aware of what they intended, surely his anger would have been continuous? If I know that a man is planning to rape a child, will I remain kindly toward him, and not show anger until the deed is actually done? Can the words, say, of Hosea, which read like a spontaneous response to what God observes on earth, contain any real passion if the Lord had known for aeons what Israel would do? –

> *How can I give you up, O Ephraim? How can I hand you over, O Israel? How can I make you like Admah? How can I treat you like*

> *Zeboiim? My heart recoils within me; my compassion grows warm and tender. (11:8, ESV)*

Likewise such statements as, *"The Lord loved the child,"* (2 Sa 12:24) suggest a spontaneous response to an event, rather than foreknowledge.

Or, I could ask, "How should the Father react to me today?" With joy because I am doing or will do well; or with anger because I am doing or will do evil? And can any of those reactions be genuine if there is no surprise in my conduct, if every impulse or action has been fully known by God millennia in advance of its happening?

So we have a choice –

- Do passages that show God responding to human action describe reality? Is God's reaction genuine and unanticipated? Does it reflect a spontaneous and immediate response to events on earth?
- Or are those scriptures engaging in a pious fiction? Must we call the divine responses a charade, since God has long before known precisely what would happen? Must we say (as some do) that the Lord is merely accommodating our ignorance by pretending to be surprised by our choices?

Numerous references show God responding in diverse ways to his people, especially in connection with his role as "husband" – delight, anger, hope, grief, pain, jealousy, admiration, disappointment, love, reward, punishment, and the like. Such emotions seem coldly artificial, unless they are indeed genuine responses to behaviour that could not be fully anticipated, or perhaps was even unexpected.

Indeed, God is frequently described in various relationships with his people –

DIVINE RELATIONS

The Lord is portrayed as being like a Husband to a wife; a Father to his children; a Judge to the lawbreakers; a Shepherd of his sheep; a King to his subjects; and others.

These relationships are all described in a context of the divine response to different sorts of human behaviour. They can have little meaning if that behaviour was already fully known by God before the people were even born. They show God as being immediately affected in heaven by what is happening on earth, and that his choices and actions are to a significant degree shaped moment by moment by what people are doing (cp. Je 3:7; 19-20).

VARIOUS RESPONSES

One of God's responses to human misbehaviour is ***"repentance"*** (119) – that is, he changes his mind about something or someone. The references are so numerous that it seems unreasonable to casually dismiss them as mere poetic accommodations. They give every impression of representing a divine reality (see Ge 6:6; 18:32; Ex 32:14; 1 Sa 15:11,35; Je 18:7-10; Ho 11:8-9; Jl 4:2; etc). Indeed, it is possible to translate the latter part of the Lord's outpouring in *Hosea 11:8* as –

---

(119) Some have claimed that the actual word "repent" is never used of God; rather, scripture says that he "relents" of having done this or that. In the context of God's responses being either artificial or spontaneous and real, I can't see that there is much difference.

> *I am so deeply moved that I have changed my mind!* [120]

Another response is to **"test"** his people, in order to discover their true character or worth (e.g. De 8:2; 13:3; Ps 66:10). Is God engaging in a pious pretence when he says to Abraham, *"Now I know that you will honour and obey me"*? (Ge 22:12) Surely the use of "now" [121] has to be misleading if the future is fully known by God? Perhaps instead scripture is simply reflecting the truth? That is, God did *not* know in advance what the result of the test would be.

Other responses are those of **"surprise"** (Je 3:7,19; 32:35; etc); or **uncertainty** (Je 26:3; 36:3; Ez 12:3; Ps 81:13. But how can God be astonished if he already knows what we will do? Or should we not take such statements seriously? Was the Lord only pretending to be surprised, or perhaps adapting his language to our ignorance? But if so, then this is a very one-sided dialogue, in which the Lord has all the advantage, while we must fumble in darkness.

Notice God's **astonishment** – *"they have built the high places of Baal to burn their sons in the fire as burnt offerings to Baal, which I did not command nor decree, **nor did it ever come into my mind** that they should do so ..."* (Je 19:5)

Or here is another striking example –

> *Therefore, the Lord God of Israel declares: I certainly thought that your family and your father's family would always live in my*

---

(120)   The passage reads literally, "Turned within me is my heart; my compassions are kindled together."

(121)   The word "now" (*attaw*) is in the Hebrew text of Genesis 22:12; it is not added by a translator.

> *presence. But now the Lord declares: I promise that I will honour those who honour me, and those who despise me will be considered insignificant." (1 Sa 2:30, GW)*

Think about the biblical warnings of punishment that will follow sin, and the promises of blessing that will follow repentance. Such passages may be understood as showing that the Lord cannot predict what the people will do. Thus, we are told that God **"*grieves*"** over our sin (Ge 6:6; Ep 4:30) and expects something better from us (Is 5:2; Je 3:6-20). Likewise, he is often described as being **"*delighted*"** when his people do well. Yet such language is surely meaningless if the Lord is already fully aware of each choice, whether good or bad, that people will make.

Another response occurs when God **"*changes his mind*"** (1 Sa 13:13; 15:11; 2 Kg 20:1-6; Je 18:-10; plus many other similar references, including places where God is said to **"*repent*"** or **"*regret*"** or **"*relent*"** previous decisions (Ge 6:6; Ex 32:14; 1 Sa 15:35; Jo 3:4; 4:2; etc). Did he change his mind, or didn't he? Are such statements only a way of humanising the Deity, making him comprehensible to us, or are they simply telling the truth? Does scripture mean what it says when, for example, it states that after Hezekiah pleaded with God *"the Lord changed his plan about the disaster he intended to bring on (Jerusalem)"*? (Je 26:19)

A COMMON OBJECTION

A common interpretation of those passages, and of others like them, is to say that they use anthropomorphic language to describe God, but don't really mean what they say. That is, whatever changes are presented should be seen as actually occurring, not in God, but in the people. God does not really "change his mind", nor his foreknowledge of events; rather, it is the people who alter their minds or actions. So then, when the Bible says that the Lord was pleased, or angry, or relented, it is simply an accommodation to our needs. It does not represent the real situation in heaven.

But that seems to be a reversal, or at least a denial, of what scripture actually says. Is our theology to be shaped by the Bible, or not? So those who hold to an "openness" view protest that statements about the Lord changing his mind or his actions are neither isolated nor few. On the contrary, there are so many such assertions scattered throughout the Old Testament that is difficult not to take them seriously. Surely, unless there is some compelling reason to do otherwise, they should be understood as rational descriptions of the actual way in which the Lord relates to his people?

I do not mean that there are no anthropomorphic passages in the Bible, for indeed there are many, such as when the Lord is described as having hands, feet, eyes, ears, and the like. Some of those places are perfectly clear, and no one would dream of taking them literally – that is, no one would suppose that the Lord God does possess physical parts, or any parts at all, in the human sense of the word. But many other places are far from clear.

Those who hold to the classical view on prescience say that they must *all* be read anthropomorphically. They deny that God can ever be taken by surprise, or that he can ever be unaware of what is to happen in either the near or the distant future. In any case, they say, God does not live in the past, the present, or the future, but rather in a wholly different dimension that is beyond time. He is like the hub of a wheel, from which the entire rim can be clearly seen. For him *all* time, from beginning to end is totally knowable and known.

Those who hold to the openness view insist rather that no matter what difficulties may arise, credence has to be given to plain biblical statements, especially when there are so many of them. If the Bible says that God was angry, then we may take it that he was indeed angry, and that this was an actual and valid response in heaven to some human action.

WHY THESE DIFFERENCES

Why do many scholars insist that divine omniscience must include full knowledge of every future event? I think for two reasons –

- Because they believe this doctrine is demanded by scripture.
- Because they find it intolerable to think that God is sometimes "in the dark" as much as we are.

There is much virtue in both reasons. Undoubtedly (as we have seen) many biblical passages *can* be taken to mean that God possesses infallible and total prescience. And it is indeed strange to think of God ever being taken by surprise, or caught unawares, or having to feel his way into the darkness as we must.

Against this, openness scholars insist that if God knows with absolute certainty every single thing we shall do, be, or become, then it must be at the cost of tightly controlling our every word, thought, and action. It would mean that we are incapable of deviating in the slightest degree from what God foreknows, which would seem to thwart any viable concept of human freedom of choice.

Some adopt the expedient (mentioned above) that is taken in *The Westminster Confession of Faith*. The Westminster divines insisted upon both full divine prescience and full human freedom, without making any attempt to reconcile the two – for they are surely irreconcilable.

That is a remarkable example of both eating the cake and keeping it whole! And all this without offering any explanation of how such a thing can be. Yet in the end, since scripture is unclear, perhaps it really is the best solution! Charles Wesley, for example, thought that the mysteries of redemption were inscrutable, and bade even the angels to cease their enquiries! –

> 'Tis mystery all: th'Immortal dies:
> Who can explore his strange design?
> In vain the firstborn seraph tries
> To sound the depths of love divine.
> 'Tis mercy all! Let earth adore,
> *Let angel minds enquire no more.* (122)

Others argue that the Lord merely knows whatever my *final* choice or action will be. That may push the problem further away, but still doesn't change it. If God does foreknow everything about me, then sooner or later I must reach a point where I am in conformity with that divine foreknowledge, at which point I am prevented from ever changing my mind or my conduct – or at least, I cannot do so without falsifying the knowledge of God, but that is inconceivable. Whatever God knows, he must know fully and perfectly, so that it is impossible for him to be in error on any matter.

WHAT GOD KNEW YESTERDAY

Or think about it this way. The classical concept of prescience requires that God's knowledge of all things knowable was complete, infallible, and unchangeable *yesterday*, and cannot (without destroying that infallibility)

---

(122) Psalms and Hymns (1738), *And Can it Be*, 2nd. stanza. Italics mine.

be changed by any action of mine *today*. But that surely removes from me any possibility of free choice?

If the Lord infallibly saw yesterday what I will do today, then I *must* do what the Lord infallibly foresaw that I would do. The one thing I cannot do is make God wrong!

Yet my daily experience tells me otherwise. I cannot doubt that I am free to do this or that, to make this decision or another, to go here or there. So the dilemma is this: either my actions today are pre-determined by what God knew yesterday, and I am not truly free; or, yesterday at least some aspects of the future were unknown to God, and I am truly free today to make whatever choices I please, which then, and *only then*, become part of God's knowledge.

DIVINE IMMUTABILITY?

Another objection is raised against the openness view – "What about scriptures that describe God as changeless, eternally the same, or '***immutable***'?" Immutability is certainly true of God's ***existence*** (he cannot cease to exist) and ***character*** (he is always ruled by love, holiness, truth, and justice). But can it be equally applied either to God's ***actions*** (which scripture says do change, cp. De 29:24; Is 28:21; Je 30:14; La 3:33); or his ***experience*** (which is shaped day by day by human behaviour, so that he is said to experience a gamut of emotions, or at least of responses to what people do)? [123]

So the matter remains indeterminate. Each side has a strength of argument. Each side remains unconvinced by the

---

(123) You will find further comment on "immutability" in Meditation # 21 below; and see also my comments on "impassibility" in # 12.

other. I suppose it is rather like the quarrel between Arminianism (with its emphasis on human freewill) and Calvinism (with its emphasis on divine sovereignty). No one has ever resolved that argument to everyone's satisfaction, nor is ever likely to do so until Jesus comes. I am inclined toward Calvin's views, but I would hardly call myself a Calvinist, for I retain a large measure of belief in the contention of Arminius, that we are free to say "No!".

Likewise, in the present debate, I incline toward the openness view, but I cannot and will not ignore the many scriptures that support the classical view of omniscience. And I ask, "Why do so many scholars feel obliged to force the Bible into a coherence that it does not possess?" On the issue of omniscience, as on several other issues, the Bible does *not* present a unified dogma, but leaves open several different options, each true in its own place.

I like what I once read somewhere, that when confronted with an anxious Christian, unsure of his or her eternal salvation, a preacher should emphasise Calvin's dogmas on the eternal security of the believer, and on the perseverance of the saints. But when faced with an arrogant or self-confident Christian, the same preacher should emphasise Arminian dogma on the risk of losing salvation unless one remains truly humble, trusting, and obedient.

So at one and the same time, I delight in thinking that the Lord God has invited me to participate with him in shaping the future; but I also delight in believing that the future is not wholly hidden from him, and that I can hold his hand and walk confidently ahead, knowing that he is in control. For while tomorrow is unknown to me, it is not so to him; and while *my* hand may be inept, *his* is irresistibly sure.

NINETEEN

PROPHECY

> O God, the Rock of Ages,
> Who evermore hast been,
> What time the tempest rages,
> Our dwelling place serene:
> Before Thy first creations,
> O Lord, the same as now,
> To endless generations,
> The everlasting Thou. [124]

Proponents of the classical view on **_omniscience_** like to point to the ability of the biblical prophets to speak oracles about future events. Surely this is a demonstration of God's complete knowledge of the future?

However, we can make several observations –

CONDITIONAL ORACLES

Many prophecies are conditional – that is, whether or not blessing or cursing will occur depends upon the people. But if God already knows what choices they will make, then the oracles are pointless. They become merely a theoretical statement of possibilities of which the Lord already knows the outcome. They cannot truly express what was in God's mind at the time.

In opposition to this, *Isaiah 46:9-11* is often quoted –

---

[124]   O God, the Rock of Ages, by Edward H. Bickersteth; 1862.

> *I am God, and there is no other like me. I declare the end from the beginning, and from ancient times I have revealed things that have not yet happened. My purpose cannot be thwarted, and what I decree, I will do. ... All that I have spoken, I will do; all that I have planned, I will fulfil.*

But surely, as the passage itself says, this future knowledge is firmly connected with what God himself has decreed, not with some foreknowledge of decisions that people will make? The same may be said of other similar affirmations, especially messianic oracles. That is, whatever God has decreed he will most certainly accomplish, but that does not mean that he has decreed the entire future (despite what the composers of the *Westminster Confession* wrote). Indeed, the decrees of God do not seem to encompass the entire future, but are mostly concerned with Christ, the Church, and the coming Kingdom. Thus Paul –

> *God has revealed the mystery of his plan to us, that is, the inheritance he has appointed us to receive through Christ. He plans to bring all history to its consummation in Christ, so that Christ will be the head of everything in heaven and on earth. From the very beginning God planned to choose us through Christ, and in his plan everything will work out just the way he has decreed. (Ep 1:9-11)*

Other prophecies are based upon trends that God can observe, and which must lead to certain inevitable outcomes.

With rare exceptions, the various oracles in both Old and New Testaments are expressed in terms sufficiently general and often shadowy, to show that they are based upon an imperfect vision – certainly on the part of the prophet, if not the Lord. This is true even of the great *Olivet Discourse* spoken by Jesus. [125] The meaning of different segments of the *Discourse* are often clear enough, but no one has ever yet succeeded in turning it into a coherent description of future events, stated in proper sequence, and with certainty about the when and how of their fulfilment. Even the great Augustine, in the early 5th century, was obliged to admit that he could not unravel the mysteries of the *Discourse*. When it deals with things that God has decreed, it speaks with great clarity. But when it deals with matters that are contingent upon human choices it speaks with wondrous slipperiness! If you doubt this, just read a few commentaries on it, representing the numerous schools of eschatology.

DIVINE GUIDANCE

The following paragraphs represent the *open future* viewpoint, to which I am giving some attention because it departs from orthodox teaching. I like their ideas, without being fully convinced, and I know that counter arguments can be raised. So do read with an open mind, and feel free to decide for yourself which opinion is more convincing. And be kind to those who make a different choice! In this area of dogma, as in several others, we are all of us staring through a dark glass, trying to bring coherence to a body of inadequate data.

Consider the effect upon seeking divine guidance if I claim that God knows every detail of the future. Suppose I were to find myself needing to choose between several difficult options, knowing that the wrong choice will have severe consequences. I come to the Lord in prayer, asking him what is the best choice? He looks into the future, sees me making

---

(125) See Matthew 24:3-31; Mark 13:3-27; Luke 21:7-36.

the wrong choice, and directs me to make another. But then, that will change the future that God has just seen! Yet how can that be, if God's knowledge of the future is deemed to be perfect?

Or to put it differently, God himself has to *act as if he does not know the future*, whether or not he does know it. And we too, whatever our dogma, must act the same way, for we cannot tell what each day will bring, and we cannot depend upon God alone to shape events so that no harm will be done to us, nor any loss incurred, nor any error made – for all those things frequently happen to all of us. Indeed, in most cases the responsibility for avoiding danger, living sensibly, making proper choices, is in our own hands. We cannot blame God for our follies.

Or to put it differently again. Suppose that God does have perfect prescience, still he cannot take any action that would change the future that he is presumed to know. In other words, God himself is obliged to act as if, outside of what he has decreed *shall* happen, he does not know any future event. He cannot change anything in the present because of what he sees in the future, for if he did, that would change the future – which renders the whole argument incoherent. So nothing is actually gained by affirming total divine foreknowledge of all things. We are still left to behave as if the Lord has to await events, just as we do.

Of course, the Lord *does* have complete knowledge of all that presently is, that is, of our nature, training, experience, character, dispositions, probable choices in each situation, all the forces that are presently exercising some influence over us, and on and on. (126) Undoubtedly, this enables him to

---

(126) He knows also the heart of man and its thoughts (1Sa 16:7; 1Kg 8:39; Ps 7:9; Ps 94:11; 139:2; Je 11:20; 17:9-10; 20:12; Ez
... continued on next page ....

make some very accurate forecasts! Yet it still leaves us with genuine freedom of choice, and the possibility of making future decisions that the Lord cannot predict with certainty, and to which it seems he must (and does) respond as each occasion requires.

It has been claimed that without complete knowledge of the future, the Lord could have had no certainty that any person would repent and gain salvation, and that therefore Christ might have died in vain. But even human actuarial tables, while they cannot determine the age at which any individual person may die, or from what cause, can nonetheless predict with uncanny accuracy how many people in a particular age group will perish in a certain way. It would be incredible if the Lord, having created us, could not know with certainty that there would always be some, if only a remnant, who would respond to his gracious invitation.

THE POWER OF PRAYER

The words of James, *"You do not receive because you do not ask,"* imply that there are things the Lord desires to give us, or situations he is willing to change, yet cannot do so because we have failed to ask for them. Surely this is because we live in a world where God has created us with genuine freedom of choice, and in doing so has voluntarily limited his own

---

11:5). Furthermore, God knows man entirely in all his ways (Ps 139:1-5; Pr 5:21). He looks from heaven and sees all men (Ps 11:4; 14:2; 33:13-15). Evil and sin are also known to God (Ge 3:11; 6:5, 6:9, 13; 2 Sa 7:20; Ps 69:5; Je 16:17; 18:23). In a word, God knows with absolute accuracy all about man (Jb 11:11; 34:21; Ps 33:15; Pr 5:21; Ho 5:3; Je 11:20; 12:3; 17:9 f.; 18:23). This perfect knowledge finds its classic expression in Ps 139. (ISBE)

freedom of action. Therefore he cannot ensure (unless he denies his own fiat) that nothing is done except what he himself desires or would prefer. Indeed, many things happen that leave the Lord, as scripture itself says, disappointed, angry, or grieved.

We can escape this problem only by accepting that what God truly prefers is a world in which even he must accept things that are not what he would choose to happen if the choice were his alone. Except that it is by his own choice that this is so!

Hence, we are free to ask or not ask, and God must ordinarily restrain his responses to conform with our prayers.

Of course, nothing can prevent the Lord from intervening in human affairs when his purpose so requires, nor from ensuring, in whatever way is morally allowable, that his ultimate will is done. But ordinarily the Lord does not interfere with our decisions and actions, and must wear the consequences of human behaviour as we must do ourselves.

This genuine freedom of choice, which is ours by divine decree, seems to me to demand a capacity to make decisions of which the Lord actually has no prior knowledge. For if the future is fully known by God, then the future is fixed; he already knows what I will or will not pray for, and what his response will be. But then my belief that I am truly free to change my mind at any time would seem to be negated.

It is little help to argue that God knows that I will change my mind, and that that is the future he knows, because that still removes from me the right to change it again independently of God's presumed foreknowledge. I become locked into the divine prescience and cannot escape its thrall.

Any kind of petition for the Lord to alter some situation on earth surely loses meaning if it does not pre-suppose that our prayers do provoke God to action that he would not have taken if we had not prayed. But any definition of omniscience that involves an absolute knowledge of the future robs such prayers of spontaneity and reduces them to an inescapable conformity to some pre-ordained destiny.

The ordinary view of omniscience turns time into something like a model railway track, where the observer can see the whole layout, and knows in advance where the train will be at any particular time. Yet I cannot feel when I pray that am I running along a track that was laid out before the eyes of God aeons ago. Time is not a line running from "A" to "B"; the past does not exist, except in memory; the future does not exist, except in anticipation. The only thing that actually exists is the present passing moment, and my perception is that I really am free, at any of those moments, to change direction, to choose a different path, to make an unexpected choice. That is, instead of using the analogy of a model railway to picture my condition, I would rather liken myself to the kind of toy that runs free when it is put on the floor, and may turn in any direction, unless guided in some way by its owner.

TWENTY

PROVIDENCE

> When wilt thou save the people?
> O God of mercy, when?
> The people, Lord, the people,
> Not thrones and crowns, but men!
> Flowers of thy heart, O God, are they;
> Let them not pass like weeds away
> Their heritage a sunless day
> God save the people
>
> When wilt thou save the people?
> O God of mercy, when?
> The people, Lord, the people!
> Not thrones and crowns, but men!
> God save the people; thine they are,
> Thy children as thy angels fair;
> From vice, oppression and despair,
> God save the people! [127]

On the matter of divine guidance that occupied part of my previous meditation, we may affirm that God knows –

- all that has happened in the past
- all that is happening in the present, including our very thoughts

---

(127) <u>Hymn</u>, Ebenezer Elliott (1850).

- all that has been made inevitable (unless he chooses to intervene) by what has happened and is happening now
- all that lies in his decree and that he has resolved will happen
- all that will probably happen, along with alternative outcomes, based on an exhaustive understanding of human nature, probabilities, cause and effect, etc.
- all else that is knowable, but not the future, except in the manner just defined.

It seems to me that only on the basis of such a definition is it reasonable to seek guidance from the Father. Genuine immediate divine guidance is hardly available if our pathway and actions are already fixed in the foreknowledge of God, for his foreknowledge of what we will choose, speak, do, and be, precludes him from taking any action that would alter that foreknowledge. Only on the view that the future is, at least to some degree, *open*, and that we are invited to enter into partnership with the Lord in shaping that future in the best possible way, can there be any reason to seek the wisdom, guidance, and direction of the Lord.

But now we come to a different problem –

THE PRESENCE OF EVIL

The question is often raised, "How can God prevent his will from ever being thwarted unless he minutely controls every single happening?"

Yet as we have seen, such a state seems to make nonsense of any claim to possess free will, or of any power in prayer to change anything. Also, if God does so control every event that it can never deviate from the future he supposedly already knows, then that would seem to make God an accessory not only to the best of virtue but also to the worst of vice.

Yet on the other hand, insofar as God (who is well able to prevent any crime from being done) fails to do so, he is already at least to some extent a partner in that crime! Even our human law courts consider someone at least partly guilty of a crime if, being able to prevent it, that person refuses or fails to do so. What then shall we say about God?

The answer seems to lie in supposing that the Lord is usually restrained by his own decree from intervening too much in human affairs. He mostly allows circumstances to work out, whether for good or ill, according to ordinary time and chance (Ec 9:11-12). Except that other decrees of God do stand above the tempests of humanity, and will infallibly be done in the time he has appointed.

SERVING SOME GREATER GOOD?

The presence of evil in the world, especially when it is extreme, seems to demand some concept of general freedom of choice for humans; that is, that God does not ordinarily interfere in human affairs, but allows people both to make and to suffer the consequences of their own choices. The argument that every instance of pain, loss, torture, war, etc., is part of an inscrutable plan of God, and will result in a greater good than could otherwise have been gained, seems intolerable. [128]

---

(128) I am speaking here of individual horrific happenings, not the general existence of pain. I freely accept that in the providence of God the present world is inevitable; it is the consequence of the freedom of choice fallen man still possesses. Out of universal suffering, God will in time bring the greater good of his Kingdom. *... continued on next page ....*

I don't doubt that there are many situations in which God is able to work for the advantage of his people. But what "greater good" can be served by an infant burning to death in a car accident, or small boys and girls being raped, or thousands of people dying of starvation, being swept away in a flood, massacred in war, or slaughtered by suicide bombers, and the like?

What shall we say about Vlad the Impaler (c. 1433-1476), who "by 1462, when he was deposed, had killed, principally by means of public impaling on stakes, many tens of thousands of his own people." (129) On occasion he impaled entire families, after stripping them naked, and beginning with the youngest child, thrusting them one by one onto sharpened stakes, where they died writhing and shrieking in unspeakable torment.

Or think about Simon de Montfort, who in March 1210, conquered the village of Bram in Languedoc. He took 100 of the villagers, men, women, and children, gouged out their eyes and cut off their ears, noses, and lips. One man was left with one eye to guide the ghastly company to the next fortress (Cabaret), in an effort (which failed) to terrify the defenders into surrender. We are not told what happened to the wretched mutilated victims of his ruthless savagery, but I doubt they could see much value in their futile misery. Then in 1210, at Minerve, Simon had 140 Cathars burned at the stake, the largest number at one time in history. The

---

But in the particular instances mentioned above, and countless others like them, it is impossible to descry any virtue or benevolent value. This idea is taken up and expounded further a few paragraphs below.

(129) Microsoft ® Encarta ® 2006. © 1993-2005 Microsoft Corporation. All rights reserved. Article *in loc*.

following year, over several months, nearly 400 Cathars were burned to death at his command.

But then, the Bible itself describes equal horrors –

> *Now Nahash, king of the Ammonites, had been grievously oppressing the Gadites and the Reubenites. He would gouge out the right eye of each of them and would not grant Israel a deliverer. No one was left of the Israelites across the Jordan whose right eye Nahash, king of the Ammonites, had not gouged out. (1 Sa 10:27b, NRSV and some other translations; plus 11:2).*

And of course the human story is drenched with the blood of millions more who died terribly, screaming their lives away in some hideous torture chamber, burnt to ashes at the stake, broken horribly on the wheel, torn asunder, or put to death in whatever dire form the depraved minds of savage rulers could devise.

It is impossible to see any redemptive value in such fathomless pain, in people so crazed with agony that they would confess to any crime, curse God wildly, do anything, say anything, just to bring their torment to an end.

In the end, the only acceptable explanation of universal suffering is that God has chosen to give freedom to his creatures, to allow them to make their own choices, and to interfere only as much as is necessary to achieve his ultimate purpose. It is evident, too, that although our tears grieve the Lord (cp Je 19:5; etc), and he wishes that their causes did not happen, he is nonetheless bound by his own decree not to interfere unless his purpose so requires. So Paul is released from prison by an earthquake, but James is brutally put to death.

Indeed, the grief, dismay, anger, horror, the Lord expresses in many places has meaning (as I have suggested above), only if he did not have prior exhaustive knowledge of what was to happen. I don't know how people who hold to the idea of total prescience can overcome this moral dilemma, except by copying the Westmister divines and simply ignoring it.

EVANGELISM

Peter once wrote about God's desire for everyone to come into union with Christ –

> *God is patient for your sake. He doesn't want to destroy anyone, but wants all people to have an opportunity to turn to him and change the way they think and act. (2 Pe 3:9, GW; and cp. 1 Ti 2:1-4)*

This seems to demand a limited knowledge of the future, and that the Lord does not know just how many will be saved. Thus too the question Jesus asked, *"Will I find faith on the earth?"* It seems to imply that he could not be sure of the answer. He knew that some would remain faithful, but not how many.

Does this give a greater motive for evangelism? Probably not, unless one is so committed to total prescience that it induces a sense of fatalism. Calvinistic Christians, unless they hold to an extreme position, are not less noticeably keen on winning souls than are Arminian Christians. Neither are those who hold to the idea of an open future likely to be any more enthusiastic servants of God than those who believe that the future is fully seen by God.

SOME CONCLUSIONS

No matter how we solve these problems, any definition of divine omniscience must include –

WHAT GOD DOES NOT KNOW

God cannot know anything that is not a proper object of knowledge, or which does not lie within the limits of knowledge fixed by his own decree. As Sirach said in the quote above, he knows "whatever is knowable" – but not even God can know what is **unknowable.**

But does this limitation apply to contingent events in the future, and if so, how? That is, is the future knowable, and if so, to what extent?

THE REAL FUTURE

As we have seen, scripture affirms that God does know at least some parts of the future (cp. Is 44:7-8, 25-28). But can he know every detail of the future (as Augustine and the Westminster divines asserted) when the future does not yet exist? Is such knowledge compatible with human freedom of choice?

Thus, contrary to Sirach, a later Jewish writer gave a list of 21 attributes of God, but omitted *foreknowledge*, preferring the term *"all-surveying"* (Wis 7:22-23. REB). He then said that "wisdom (God) knows the things of old, and **infers** the things to come" (8:8, emphasis mine). That is, God's knowledge of the future differs from his knowledge of the past. It is less certain, because at least to some degree it is contingent upon the free choices that men and women make day by day.

Theologians have quarrelled about this question endlessly over the centuries, and the matter remains unresolved, for we seem to be locked into a dilemma: either we stress human freedom of choice at the expense of divine foreknowledge; or the reverse.

Perhaps the best solution lies in the suggestion made here that parts of the future are fixed, and are therefore fully known by God, whereas other parts are still open and depend as much upon human choice as upon God's. A dramatic example of this viewpoint can be found in a group of oracles where God furiously condemns nations who went beyond his purpose in oppressing Israel. We can notice

- ***first***, that the prophets predicted the judgment that God had said would fall upon his rebellious people – so in that sense the Lord was aware of the future, even in some detail. But then,
- **second**, the nations who were supposed to be no more than a *"hammer in the hand of God"* to punish Israel, instead acted with a terrible savagery that far exceeded the mandate they had been given – see Isaiah 10:5-12; 37:21-22,28-29; 47:5-6; and note the remarkable sentiment in Jeremiah 42:10c (*"I am sorry for the disaster that I have brought upon you!"*); and in Zechariah 1:14-15 (*"I was angry with those nations, but now I am enraged, because they have treated Jerusalem far worse than I intended!"*)

The most natural reading of those scriptures, and of others like them, seems to require a blending of divine foreknowledge with an open future. That is, God knows the future so far as it has been fixed by his own decrees and by his vast wisdom and his deep knowledge of both the present scene, of current trends, and of human nature. But where the future still depends upon certain human decisions, then it remains at least to some degree open and flexible.

Thus we need to think about –

THE POTENTIAL FUTURE

Think once again about the gaps in Jesus' *Olivet Discourse*, and the fragmentary nature of Bible prophecy in general. Think about passages like *Jeremiah 18:6-10*, which seem to declare an open and variable future –

> *People of Israel, I, the Lord, have power over you, just as a potter has power over clay. If I threaten to uproot and shatter an evil nation and that nation turns from its evil, I will change my mind. If I promise to make a nation strong, but its people start disobeying me and doing evil, then I will change my mind and not help them at all. So listen to me, people of Judah and Jerusalem! I have decided to strike you with disaster, and I won't change my mind unless you stop sinning and start living right. (CEV)*

We ought to be able to take such an oracle at face value; that is, God is plainly conditioning his future actions upon the actions of the people. If the Lord already knew what each nation will choose, then the oracle must lack both passion and sincerity.

So, for example, can even God say (other than potentially) what might have happened if Nebuchadnezzar had not made his heroic and extraordinary dash across the desert to claim his throne; or what would happen if 2+2 in Euclidian arithmetic were to equal 5; or what might have been if you or I had not been born?

Yet there are those who argue the contrary, namely, that God does and must have complete and perfect knowledge not only of this world but of all potential worlds.

Like the unresolvable tension between human freedom of will and divine predestination, this problem of omniscience may be finally insoluble – perhaps it lies beyond the reach of human intellect, and we should probably be content to assert only

- that our future is assuredly open, and
- that God assuredly knows all that can be known about it!

Anything more than that is dogma, which may or may not be true.

WHAT GOD DOES KNOW

AS WE HAVE SEEN ALREADY, HE KNOWS EVERYTHING THAT LIES WITHIN THE PROPER BOUNDS OF KNOWLEDGE.

That certainly means everything that actually has been, is, and (at least) such elements of the future as

- are fixed by his own decree (Ro 9:10-13);
- can be firmly predicted on the basis of known law; or
- are knowable.

In addition, scholars like to affirm that God's knowledge is intuitive not discursive, immediate not sequential, total not partial, conscious not hidden. But whether such claims, logical as they may be, represent the truth is another matter. They have more the sound of rational dogma than of biblical necessity.

But we can affirm that God has a total, present, immediate, vivid awareness of everything that can be perceived or known (He 4:13; Ps 139:11-12; Pr 15:3,11; Je 23:24). Yet this does not prevent him from being able to focus or remove attention at his own discretion (Ma 3:16-17; Is 49:15-16; He 8:12). Nor does it prevent some kind of sequence occurring within the divine mind. Scripture asserts that God thinks, reasons, argues, and the like, which seem to demand that even in the mind of God thoughts must follow each other, as they do in our minds. But how this can be remains a mystery.

FOREKNOWLEDGE AND PREDESTINATION

Foreknowing is not the same as foreordaining. Some things are predetermined by God; they are numbered amongst his decrees. Other things are simply known by God (but how far this knowledge extends, as we have seen, is a matter of debate).

He knows our present thoughts (Ps 139:2); the future (at least insofar as he has decreed it, Is 46:8-11); and everything about us (Is 29:15-16).

Despite all the mysteries and debates, I will say these things with certainty –

Whatever God *needs* to know, he knows, whether in the past, the present, or the future. It is unthinkable that lack of knowledge of what may happen, or is about to happen, or will happen in the future, should ever inhibit the power of God to do whatever he pleases. If necessary, he will decree the future, and achieve it, yet without in any way denying his own nature or diminishing the freedom of choice he has given us. Therefore, also –

- Whatever knowledge our salvation requires, God knows it; and
- Whatever knowledge the mind of God must hold to guide us safely from earth to glory, and to secure our possession of Paradise, God has it; and
- Whatever knowledge God must possess in order to bring his church to its glorious destiny as the Bride of Christ, God possesses it.

TWENTY-ONE

IMMUTABLE

> Hail, Father, whose creating call
> Unnumbered worlds attend;
> Jehovah, comprehending all,
> Whom none can comprehend!
> Thy name, Jehovah, be adored
> By creatures without end,
> Whom none but thy essential Word
> And Spirit comprehend. [130]

The Lord God is said to be **_immutable_** – that is, unchanging, the same always and everywhere in his *nature, character,* and *purpose.* Since God is already absolutely perfect in every possible way, he cannot change, either for better or worse; he is the same today as he was yesterday, and will always be the same (He 13:8).

Does this mean that God is unfeeling, lacking passion (as the old divines claimed)? [131]

---

(130) From Poems on Several Occasions (1736), St. 1 & 6; by Samuel Wesley Jr.

(131) The 1646 Westminster Confession of Faith says, "There is but one only living and true God, who is infinite in being and perfection, a most pure spirit, invisible, without body, parts, or passions, immutable, immense, eternal, incomprehensible, almighty, most wise, most holy, most free, most absolute ..." (emphasis mine). The statement that God has no passions may be pious, but it has a sound of dogmatic folly rather than good sense.

No, for "immutability" cannot mean that God is static, unfeeling, or incapable of emotional change. Rather, it applies to his unchanging consistency. That is, he will never act in a manner that opposes his other attributes of holiness, justice, goodness, wisdom, love, and the like. His purpose remains resolute; his word remains trustworthy (Ja 1:17); his character remains unchanging and unchangeable (Ps 102:25-28). He is therefore wholly dependable.

Nonetheless, God's *actions* can change and be changed, and also his *relationships*, as he responds to the choices made by his creatures in the exercise of the free will he has himself given them. This explains some seeming contradictions in scripture –

- Thus, James tells us that there is no variableness in God – he never casts a shifting shadow – (1:17), but Stephen says that there are times when God does *"turn away"* from his people (Ac 7:42).
- Balaam cried that God is not like a man who tells lies, or changes his mind (Nu 23:19), but the Psalmist says that *"God remembered his promise to (Israel), and in keeping with his rich mercy, he changed his plans"* (106:44-45, GW).

The changes described in passages like those do not take place in the fundamental character, purpose, or promise of God, but only in his relationship to his creatures, based upon the extent of their obedience or trust. They reflect changes in his *works* not in his will, in his *actions* not in his essence.

So God's immutability is not inert, but dynamic; it is not that of an endlessly frozen and infinitely beautiful statue, but refers only to his moral character, his purposes, his justice, and his promises, which remain unchanging through all the fluctuations of time, chance, and circumstance. Immutability does not indicate an immobile sameness, but a dynamic constancy, the impossibility of deviating from the best.

Likewise, it does not mean that God is not flexible, but that in everything he says and does he is entirely consistent with himself. So he can respond to human behaviour with either love or anger, blessing or disaster, but each response is true to his own unchanging nature.

Immutability does not fetter God's creativity nor preclude infinite variety in his works, which is evident from the dazzling wonders of creation that surround us on our dusty planet and stretch out to the furthest limits of space.

Every attribute of God is dependent upon his immutability, for if God does change then we cannot rely on either his character or his promises, whereas we know that we may place total confidence in all that he has ever spoken and will ever do.

This attribute is impossible for any contingent being, that is, for any creature. Yet by a wonderful paradox the glory of God is revealed in *us* through a process of *endless change* and advance! (Is 9:7; 2 Co 3:17-18)

And somewhere I found the following list, which shows that immutability is affirmed of God's –

- ***essence*** (Jb 23:13; cp He 13:8)
- ***character*** (Ps 102:25-27)
- ***attributes*** (Ma 3:6; Ps 7:11-12)
- ***purposes*** (Ps 33:11; Is 46:9-10; Tit 1:2-3)
- ***promises*** (1 Pe 1:23-25).

INFINITY

God is said to be ***infinite*** – that is, having neither beginning nor end, invisible, eternal, spiritual (Jn 4:24), unbounded by time, space, or any physical parts. He inhabits eternity, not time, and he is unrestrained by any limitations except that he cannot grow any larger nor increase in any way at all, for he is already infinite. So, apart from the fact that he cannot ever be less or more than infinite, he is curtailed only by his own nature and will.

Some have argued that if God is infinite then he must include within himself every possible thing and every mode of being, which results in a kind of pantheism. But the argument is fallacious. We can imagine several infinite things existing independently of each other – such as the infinite series of numbers, or the infinite reaches of space. We can also imagine an infinite thing dwelling apart from a finite thing – for example, the infinite love of God alongside the restricted love of man. Because God is infinite we cannot avoid *"living, moving, and having our being in him"* (Ac 17:28); but we are nonetheless distinct beings, with a distinguishable consciousness.

In relation to *space*, God's infinity is called **omnipresence**. In relation to *action*, God's infinity is called **omnipotence**. In relation to *time*, God's infinity is called **eternity**.

What is eternity? Not just endless time, for space and time are created things. They are finite, and they cannot place any restraint upon God who, while he is everywhere present in the universe, still dwells apart from time and space. In contrast with time, eternity is both the habitation of God (Is 57:15) and a divine attribute (De 33:27). Therefore it seems that we must say that there is neither past nor future with God; he has no memory of *"yesterday"*, nor any anticipation of *"tomorrow"*; he possesses the whole of his past, present, and future in one indestructible, indivisible, immeasurable moment (cp. Jn 8:58; 2 Pe 3:8).

Perhaps we may infer from this that God must see what to us is the *future* as clearly as he sees the *present* and the *past* ? And there are some who so argue. But the idea is difficult –

as I have tried to show above – and perhaps we must simply concede that the mystery is impenetrable by the human mind. Indeed, we cannot form a realistic mental picture of any boundless object, whether natural or divine, for we are obliged to live within a fence of time and place. No matter how far we count, we cannot grasp the infinite series of numbers, nor can we conceive the infinite dimensions of love, nor wrap our minds around the infinity of God. In a sense we know what we mean when we talk about eternity and infinity, but they defy verbal description; we "feel" them much better than we can explain them!

We can more easily say what eternity is *not* than what it is – eternity is that which has no beginning, no end, no succession of parts nor of moments; it is simply *now*. Yet such a statement leaves us unsatisfied, even if we cannot do any better. Likewise with *infinity* – we say it is that which has no boundaries, but just what that means constantly escapes our grasp.

TIME IS A CREATED THING

Notice that *"time"* is inextricably bound up with the physical creation; time began when the world began, and it will end when the world ends. At once we face another thicket of thorns! The relation of time to eternity is one of the most difficult problems in philosophy and theology. Just as we struggle to comprehend infinity so we are baffled by time. As Augustine said, we know exactly what time is, until we are asked to explain it! Is it just something our human minds perceive, a matter of memory, of awareness, of anticipation; or does it really exist? (See the following meditation for further comment on "time".)

"Time" is the passing away of some things and the coming into existence of others; we are aware of time only because we remember the past, exist in the present, and anticipate

the future. If there were no such consciousness there would be no time, or at least no sense of time (Is 65:17) –

> *I am going to create a new heaven and a new earth in which nothing from the past will be remembered; it will not even come to mind.*

That cessation of *"memory"* beyond the grave and in the new world, may indicate a partial grasp of *"eternity"*; but not wholly, because presumably we will always possess anticipation. In fact we can and do touch *"eternity"* in our *minds* already – we can *"hear"* an entire symphony in a moment of memory, or visualise in a flash all the features of a long journey, or touch in an instant the most distant galaxy, or see in a single vision our whole life. In a sense, the present moment is a footprint on the very edge of eternity, it is the point at which time begins to fuse with eternity. Thus God has made it possible for us to conceive eternity, but only partially. For us there will probably always be a sense of dwelling in a vivid moment at the centre of eternity past and present (cp Ec 3:11, NIV; and note the locus at the centre of the expression, *"from everlasting |to| everlasting,"* [Ps 41:13; 90:2]). We will live where the "to" stands, and in some ways do so already.

Because we are and always will be contingent beings, our junction with eternal life must always be other than God's possession of it. It seems impossible to imagine a situation in which we shall lose all sense of the future; yet it also seems appalling to imagine the future as nothing more than endless time! No pleasure could ever survive the exhaustion of aeons upon aeons of time, following one upon the other for ever and ever. In the end, as finite beings presently locked into time and space, eternity lies beyond our grasp. It is simply too foreign to our present mode of existence. We know it is the realm in which God dwells; we know that in some measure we will share it; but we cannot truly define it.

However, our eternal wellbeing is secure in the promise of God (1 Jn 5:11-13). As the Grand Inquisitor says in *The Gondoliers,*

> Of that there is no manner of doubt
> No probable, possible shadow of doubt
> No possible doubt whatever! (132)

Finally in this meditation, perhaps we may better define *"eternal life"*, not with a sense of duration, nor even of endlessness, but rather in the sense of a particular quality of life, a perfection of life in *"eternity"*, the realm in which God has his habitation, the place of Paradise, the place of our destination in the everlasting Kingdom of God.

---

(132)   Opera by Gilbert and Sullivan, *Act One*; first performed in 1889.

TWENTY-TWO

TIMELESS

> Praise to the living God!
> All praisèd be his Name,
> Who was, and is, and is to be,
> For aye the same.
> The one eternal God
> Ere aught that now appears –
> The first, the last, beyond all thought,
> His timeless years!
>
> Eternal life hath he
> Implanted in the soul;
> His love shall be our strength and stay
> While ages roll.
> Praise to the living God!
> All praisèd be his Name,
> Who was, and is, and is to be,
> For aye the same. (133)

"Beyond all thought, his timeless years!" cried the poet, and expressed the fathomless mystery of time. God is **_timeless_**, yet in a sense he must dwell in the same years that encompass us while also inhabiting eternity (Is 57:15). So let us continue our exploration of the conundrum of time, (134)

---

(133) From a Jewish doxology, translated by Max Landsberg and Newton Mann, 1914.

(134) The next couple of pages are an expansion of some thoughts that can also be found in my book When the Trumpet Sounds, Chapter Three – Excursus.

even though the timeless years of God truly *are* "beyond all thought", existing in a realm that we cannot fully comprehend.

We should perhaps begin by trying to see time as God sees it. He is not under time's compulsion, as we are. He made time, and must reckon with it; but he is not its prisoner. This is admittedly an enigma, but Peter expresses it simply in the saying: *"One day is to the Lord a thousand years, and a thousand years is one day!"* How that can be, who can tell? We are time-bound; God is eternal, and it might seem that the two can never meet. Yet in Christ, God *has* invaded time; and through Christ we are being brought into *eternity*.

Let us search out what we can of this puzzle, beginning with the riddle of the **past**. Long ago John Donne wrote the lines –

> Go, and catch a falling star,
> Get with child a mandrake root,
> Tell me where all past years are,
> Or who cleft the Devil's foot ... (135)

"Tell me where all past years are?" the bard demanded, and voiced one of the greatest mysteries of human experience. What happened to the world that existed just a moment ago? This present world is not the same as the one that was here in the past second. But where did that one *go*? And from where does the world come that we shall enter in the next moment? The world's deepest thinkers have been baffled by the mystery of time. Even Solomon had to admit ignorance –

> *God has made everything to harmonise with its own time; thus he has given to men and*

---

(135) The opening lines of John Donne's 18th century poem, *Go, and Catch a Falling Star*.

> *women an awareness of the passage of time. Yet they are unable to grasp how God's work begins, nor how it will end. (Ec 3:11).*

In our science, time is joined with space as one of the two basic building blocks of the universe. Nonetheless, as far as we know, in the entire universe we humans alone are conscious of time. Even on Earth time is a concept found only in fairly advanced cultures; among primitives it has no meaning, and often their languages lack any past tense. Primitive peoples appear to live – as do other sensate beings – in a kind of timeless present. Thus time is an abstract riddle that exists only in certain human minds; it has no concrete reality of its own. The only thing that actually exists is the present moment advancing inexorably toward the moment that has arrived, vanished, and merged into another even as you read these words.

In our culture, time is a familiar measuring tool. But what are we measuring? We all know what it is – until somebody asks us to explain it! We *sense* what time is much better than we can *show* what it is! Thus **_Augustine_** asked (c. 400 A.D.) –

> "What is time? Who can easily and briefly explain it? Who can ever begin to understand it, let alone speak a sensible word about it! Yet in daily conversation there is nothing we refer to more familiarly and knowingly than time. We know just what we mean when we speak about time, and we know what others mean when they speak about time to us. What then is time? If no-one asks me, I know; but if I am

asked to explain time, then I no longer know." (136)

Time is essentially a perception of movement. But from what, to what?

- **_The past has no existence_**, except in our memories. Think what it would mean if the past did retain some kind of substantial existence. Everyone would be condemned for ever to keep on doing endlessly everything they have ever done! Somewhere in that past you would not only be repeating all your previous actions, but you would be implacably moving toward doing again all the things that you were yet to do, right up until the last moment. And as each new moment creates a new past, so the entire process would be starting again, and again, and again. It is too horrific to contemplate! Happily for us, the past is nothing but a memory. Perhaps captured in print and picture, but having no real existence. So any thought of travel back into the past is just fiction. Indeed, if the future and the past are real, and time travel were possible, people from the future would already be visiting our planet, coming back to us from, say, the 25th century to see what life was like in the 21st. (137) But of course –

- **_The future has no existence_**, except in our imagination, or in our anticipation of it. We have only the present moment, which we cannot find any way to grasp. Not even our clocks can seize the present. They show us, not what the time is now, but what it was an

---

(136) Confessions, Bk 11.14.17; paraphrase mine.
(137) See *Addendum Number IV* below for a further comment on time travel.

instant ago. The moment you look at your watch, that moment has already slipped into the past.

The problem of the infinite divisibility of time was pondered by a 5th century BC Greek, **_Zeno of Elea_**. He wondered how a second could consist of smaller intervals, which themselves could be broken up into still smaller ones, and so on without end. Many thinkers have grappled in vain with this paradox.

Perhaps time is simply moving from the present into the present; but that doesn't make much sense, for then time would cease to exist altogether, and become eternity. Then again, perhaps that is the reality, that the present moment is simply an instant snatched out of eternity.

So **_Augustine_** again –

> I say with confidence, that I know that if nothing passed away there would not be past time; and if nothing were coming, there would not be future time; and if nothing were, there would not be present time. Those two times, therefore, past and future, how can they be, when even the past now is not, and the future is not as yet? But should the present be always present, and should it not pass into time past, time truly could not be, but eternity. (138)
>
> That I measure time, I know. But I do not measure the future, for it does not yet exist; nor do I measure the present, because it occupies no measurable space; nor do I measure the past, because it has gone out of existence.

---

(138)   Op. cit.

> What therefore do I measure? (139)
>
> In what part of space, then, do we measure passing time? Do we measure time in the future, for the present moment has come out of the future? But the future as yet does not exist, so how can we measure it? Or do we measure time in the present, through which it is passing? But neither does the present moment occupy any space – for as soon as the moment arrives, it is gone again; it lingers not at all. Or do we measure time in the past, into which it passes? But how can we measure that which has no existence, except in memory? ...
>
> My soul yearns to know this most tangled enigma ... I confess unto thee, O Lord, that I am as yet ignorant as to what time is; and again I confess unto thee, O Lord, that I know that I speak these things in time, and that I have already long spoken of time. How then do I do this, when I know not what time is? (140)

Augustine claimed that the universe and time were created together, but he saw time as a distinct entity. He disputed the idea that time is actually dependent upon the physical creation, and that it is marked by the motions of the universe. He was wrong of course, because modern science has shown the unbreakable link between the universe, time, and motion through space. (141)

---

(139)   Ibid. ch, 26.
(140)   Ibid, ch 21, paraphrased; ch 22; ch 25
(141)   City of God, ch 6; and Confessions, Bk 11.23.29.

John Hobbes (17th century English philosopher) claimed that only the present has any existence in nature; the past exists only in memory; the future has no existence at all.

William James (late 19th century American philosopher) –

> Let anyone try, I will not say to arrest, but simply to notice or attend to *the present moment*. One of the most baffling experiences occurs. Where is it, this present moment? It has melted in our grasp, fled ere we could touch it, gone in the instant of becoming! (142)

Richard P. Feynman (20th century American physicist and Nobel Laureate) –

> What is time? We physicists work with it every day, but don't ask me what it is. It's just too difficult to think about! ...

> The Western idea that past, present, and future are arranged in a straight line – that time does not repeat – seems to have grown out of a Judeo-Christian tradition, in which events like the creation and Christ's resurrection take on special meaning because they occur in a sequence. It may also lead to a belief in life after death, rather than in earthly reincarnation.

> Today when we glance at the clock and rush out the door, we are running our lives by a system of Babylonian numerology, coupled with Egyptian technology, within the framework of

---

(142) Principles Of Psychology, ch 15.

> an Old Testament creation epic – all synchronised by a technology that can split a second into unlimited pieces. ...
>
> Clocks and calendars create the illusion that we live in a world of mathematically measured segments of time. (143)

Did you notice the word "illusion"? Strange as it may seem, time truly does seem to be a construct of our particular culture, and exists only because we say that it exists. Yet without it we could hardly function, our social structure would collapse!

THE PROBLEM OF LINEAR TIME

Our concept of linear time has had a profound impact upon our culture, shaping our ideas of progress, and also (more destructively) creating in us a compulsion to cram everything possible into our lifetime, since there will be no other opportunity. Other cultures, where time is viewed as a repeating cycle, have not been driven by the same sense of urgent need to utilise effectively every moment.

Yet in reality, the only thing we can logically demonstrate is that we live in a kind of continuous flowing present, consisting of a few seconds before and behind each event. The present cannot be a hard, measurable instant, with clear boundaries. It must have a kind of "sponginess" about it, a vague definition with shadowy edges, like the diffuse borders around a romantic photo.

---

(143)   National Geographic magazine, March 1990; pg. 109,128,129.

If each moment were instantaneous, quite distinct from both the moment before and after, we would not be able to make the necessary connections between such things as words in a sentence, or notes in a piece of music. Only as we are able to connect these things one with the other can they be transformed into coherent and continuous experiences. [144] An illustration can be seen in a moving picture. If the film is still, a viewer can see the frames only one at a time. But if the film is set in motion, then suddenly everything comes to life, and the action portrayed becomes smooth and realistic.

Kahlil Gibran describes the mystery of linear time this way –

> You would measure time the measureless and the immeasurable.
>
> You would adjust your conduct and even direct the course of your spirit according to hours and seasons.
>
> Of time you would make a stream upon whose bank you would sit and watch its flowing.
>
> Yet the timeless in you is aware of life's timelessness,
>
> And knows that yesterday is but today's memory and tomorrow is today's dream.
>
> And that that which sings and contemplates in you is still dwelling within the bounds of that first moment which scattered the stars into space.
>
> Who among you does not feel that his power to love is boundless?

---

(144)   Ibid.

> And yet, who does not feel that very love, though boundless, encompassed within the centre of his being, and moving not from love thought to love thought, nor from love deeds to other love deeds?
>
> And is not time even as love is, undivided and spaceless?
>
> But if in your thought you must measure time into seasons, let each season encircle all the other seasons,
>
> And let today embrace the past with remembrance and the future with longing. (145)

In the end we must turn back to scripture, where we learn that time was created by God, who inhabits eternity, and that time is the vehicle that carries us irresistibly on into the purpose of God.

Therefore, in the economy of God there is neither delay nor haste. What may seem premature to us, is delayed to God; what seems delayed to us, is premature to God – except that, in reality, *with God everything is simply right on time!*

Hence we are called to steadfast patience (He 10:35-39). Note the conflict between *"he is coming soon"* and *"you must be patient"*; the first is spoken from God's perspective, and the second from ours. Christ will surely come at the time appointed by the Father. In the meantime we must patiently wait, even if, to us, his coming seems long delayed.

---

(145)   The Prophet; pub. Alfred A. Knopf, New York, 1968; pg. 62,63.

THE FOUR MODELS OF TIME

Across the centuries there have been four major theories about the passage of time –

THE RANDOM THEORY

This is the view of the existentialist and atheist, that every event is unplanned, unguided, unconnected, without purpose or form; a view sternly castigated in scripture (cp Je 50:45-46). It could be diagrammed as a series of random dots on a sheet without borders.

THE INFINITE THEORY

Aristotle argued for this view, by contending that every "now" implies a "before"; therefore time had no beginning, and probably will have no end. Tatian (an Assyrian apologist, c. 150 A.D.) retorted –

> Why do you Greeks divide time, saying that one part is past, and another is present, and another future? For how can the future be passing when the present exists? As those who are sailing imagine in their ignorance, as the ship is borne along, that the hills are in motion, so you do not know that it is *you* who are passing along, but that time remains present as long as the Creator wills it to exist. [146]

Tatian's argument has its own weakness, as we shall see later; but the Assyrian was certainly closer to scripture than

---

(146) *Address to the Greeks, ch. 26.* Tatian (*c.* 120-185), was an early Christian writer from Assyria.

were the Greeks. Against the ancient Greek opinion stand at least two scriptures – *Revelation 21:6; 22:13*.

The *Infinite View* of time could be diagrammed as a line extending endlessly in either direction.

THE CYCLIC THEORY

Other Greeks held the view that time is an endless repetition of identical cycles, a view that is still held by Hindus and Buddhists, and by some modern scientists. (147) Heraclitus (c. 500 B.C), for example, thought that the cycles of time were built around a cosmic year of 360 generations, which he calculated as 10,800 years, while the ancient Chinese taught a 129,800 year cycle. The 3rd century B.C. Greek Stoic philosopher Chrysippus held to this cyclic view –

> One of the great philosophers was Chrysippus (280-207 BC), who wrote some 700 books, of which only a few fragments now remain. He was a member of the Stoic school. The Stoics believed that there are certain fixed periods, that at the end of each period the world is destroyed in a great conflagration, and that then the same story in every littlest detail takes place all over again. This is how Chrysippus described it –
>
> "Then again the world is restored anew in a precisely similar arrangement as before. The

---

(147) However, as far as I know, most of the current versions of the "Big Bang" theory posit an ever-expanding universe into an infinite future. But I think that some cosmologists, at the time of this writing (2012), still hold to the view that the universe will eventually stop expanding and begin to shrink back into an infinitesimal point only to explode again, in an endless cycle.

stars move again in their orbits, each performing the same revolutions as in the former period, without any variation. Socrates and Plato and each individual man will live again, with the same friends and fellow-citizens. They will go through the same experiences and the same activities. Every city and village and field will be restored just as it was. And this restoration of the universe takes place, not just once, but over and over again – indeed to all eternity, without end!" (148)

The prophets, however, did not agree (Is 45:16-17) –

Yahweh is the Saviour of Israel, and he gives them an age-enduring salvation; throughout the ages of eternity they will never be ashamed nor confounded!

The cyclic view could be diagrammed as a perfect circle, spinning endlessly around.

THE LINEAR THEORY

This is the biblical view, and indeed, would not exist without the witness of scripture (2 Pe 3:8-9). It could be diagrammed as a straight line with a clearly marked beginning and end, except that the line is complete only to the present moment. Or perhaps we should think of it more as a group of moving dots, with each group representing the immediate past, the present moment, and the approaching moment. In any case, the process has its beginning in God, and will end with his

---

(148) William Barclay. I have lost the source of this quote, except that it comes from his Daily Study Bible –*The New Testament*; The St Andrew Press.

fiat. Time is not eternal. It began. It will end. Only God and those who are born into his family possess a quality of eternity.

So this biblical and linear view teaches that time has an origin and a terminus in the creative purpose of God. We are therefore called to live with a goal (Ph 3:13-14), and to set ourselves both to discover our proper goal in God and to press on until it has been fully achieved.

FINALE

My Pen! take pain a little space
To follow that which doth me chase,
And hath in hold my heart so sore;
But when thou hast this brought to pass,
My Pen! I prithee write no more.

Since thou hast taken pain this space
To follow that which doth me chase,
And hath in hold my heart so sore,
Now hast thou brought my mind to pass,
My Pen! I prithee write no more. [149]

---

(149)   Sir Thomas Wyatt (1503-42); first and last stanzas.

ADDENDA

SOME INSUPERABLE HURDLES

> *"You have not shown to anyone how your ways may be comprehended!" Then the angel said to Ezra, "Do you think you can comprehend the way of the Most High?" Then I said, "Yes, my lord." And he replied to me, "I have been sent to show you three ways, and to put before you three problems. If you can solve one of them for me, I also will show you the way you desire to see, and will teach you why the heart is evil." I said, "Speak on, my lord." And he said to me, "Go, weigh for me the weight of fire, or measure for me a measure of wind, or call back for me the day that is past."*
> (2 Es 2:30-3:5, RSV)

We cannot "call back the day that is past", nor weigh a flame, nor measure a breath – how then can we hope to comprehend God?

Yet, while pondering the unfitness of any fallen human to define any part of the divine being, the following ideas occurred to me.

Any consideration of the attributes of God at once faces two nearly insuperable problems. We need to be reminded of these problems, for it is easy for human arrogance to suppose it has gained some mastery <u>over</u> God simply because it has devised some axioms _about_ him. But we should be kept humble by remembering –

THE PROBLEM OF INADEQUACY

The renowned 18th century metaphysical poet John Donne wrote about the folly of trying to encompass the Infinite within the confines of finite words. One may as well try to turn even numbers into odd or change black into white, for the Lord refuses to fit into our poor definitions –

> Eternal God, for whom who ever dare
> Seek new expressions, do the circle square,
> And thrust into strait corners of poor wit
> Thee, who art cornerless and infinite.

We are at best like people looking through a piece of smoky glass, so that **all** our knowledge about God (and indeed, about _anything_) must remain fragmentary (1 Co 13:12).

In many areas of learning those shadows may not pose an insuperable problem, but the knowledge of God is a special case, for we are at risk of blasphemy if we say either too little or too much about him (cp. Ec 5:1-3).

Therefore some scholars have argued that because we cannot say _everything_ about God, we should say _nothing_. But that seems too drastic, for no-one can read the Bible without learning at least _something_ about the nature and being of the Lord.

Nonetheless, it behoves us to approach this sacred matter with all reverence and awe, humbly acknowledging our incompetence ever to scale the heights of the glory of the Almighty and Infinite Lord (Ro 3:23).

THE PROBLEM OF INCOHERENCY

We must remember that probably _everything_ we say about God must be at least to some degree _false_. [150] There are three reasons for this –

THE LIMITS OF LANGUAGE

It is impossible for finite words to comprehend an infinite deity. The most extravagant and richest words at our command can hardly even approximate the endless majesty and splendour of the Creator of all things. God is simply too big to be wrapped up in human definitions.

THE LIMITS OF MEANING

Words have at least slightly different meanings for each person who uses them, so that no one ever _fully_ understands what any of us mean by the things we say. Thus none of my hearers has ever heard the sermon I _actually_ preached, for they apply their own meanings to the words I use. Nor is it possible for mere words to convey with sufficient adequacy the emotions, feelings, passion, intensity, and other such subtle elements that underlie our speech. This is because all significant words carry along with them a quantity of freight [151] that differs from user to user. The result is that

---

(150) Consider even such a basic statement as "God is Love!" It is true, because God certainly is "love"; yet it is also false, because our best concept of the divine attribute must fall far short of its reality. Indeed, all earthly definitions of that heavenly love must fail, because the criteria we use are inescapably tainted by sin.

(151) That is, an array of associated ideas, memories, emotions, experiences, and definitions that add colour and richness to the words we use. They transcend the limitations of any dictionary, and also differ from person to person. Even simple words like
... *continued on next page* ....

perfect communication is virtually impossible, except at the simplest level.

THE LIMITS OF COMPREHENSION

Two barriers prevent people from arriving at perfect unanimity about almost anything –

THE BARRIER OF PREPARATION

We all come from different backgrounds socially, culturally, educationally, environmentally, etc., which cause us to see various things in different ways and to attach different levels of significance to them. What seems mightily important to one, can seem inconsequential to another. For example, at various times in church history Christian leaders have banned the use of musical instruments in worship, or the singing of hymns other than from the Bible. They have forbidden levying interest on loans of money, or the reading of novels. They have insisted that congregations should be segregated, with men sitting in one place, and women in another. And there have been many other practices, which now seem silly, or even barbaric, that our forefathers adamantly claimed were the will of God.

We read the Bible differently from our forefathers, and we do not condone slavery, flogging unwed pregnant girls, capital punishment for minor crimes, forcing little children to work fifteen-hour days in coal mines, burning witches to death, and the like. Yet past Christians, both Catholic and Protestant, firmly believed that they had biblical approval for all those horrors. But times have changed, and they have changed our understanding of the scriptures, just as a better

---

red, cat, beach, book, will create a different set of images in the minds of each hearer.

understanding of the scriptures has helped to change the times.

Nonetheless, despite our hopefully wiser and gentler precepts today, cultural differences still deeply, and often unconsciously, influence the way people look at and understand their Bibles. Hence full agreement on doctrine is unlikely ever to happen.

THE BARRIER OF PERSUASION

One product of the Fall is that our minds have been affected, so that arguments that one person finds convincing leave another unmoved. Thus we have fierce divisions among voters in their support of one political party rather than another, and huge differences in musical and literary taste, entertainment preferences, sporting activities, diet, and the like.

In the end we all believe a matter, not so much because we find an argument intellectually unassailable, but because we *feel* that it is right! But since those "feelings" can and do differ widely from person to person, we are all prone to accept some things readily that our neighbours reject, and to reject other things that they accept.

That is certainly one of the reasons why complete agreement among the churches on the body of Christian doctrine has so far been impossible to achieve. Christian scholars, of equal integrity and sincerity, differ widely in their notions of what the Bible teaches. Hence, one insists that there is a communication of divine grace through the sacraments, while another says that they are merely symbols. One declares that infant baptism is valid, while another insists upon baptising believing adults only. One excludes all but the initiated from the eucharist, another invites all who are willing to come. And so on it goes – debates about church government, the second coming of Christ, the manner salvation is obtained, the nature of the atonement, predestination, the future ages, and many more.

The consequence should be a humble acknowledgement of the incompleteness of our dogmas, and respect for sincerely held alternative beliefs.

Any discussion of the *"Attributes of God"* inescapably falls under the above restraints, and we should recognise that even our best efforts never carry us deeper than the merest shallows at very edge of the infinity that comprises our astounding God.

THE COSMOLOGICAL ARGUMENT

This *Proof of God*, based on a cause and effect notion, has a long and varied history, sometimes waxing mighty in the arguments of scholars, sometimes apparently dashed to pieces only, like the Phoenix, to rise again from its ashes.

In the end, all the arguments resolve to the one idea, with which everyone agrees – <u>something</u> exists that must be construed as self-caused, eternal, and infinite. But is that *something* the universe itself, or a Being (whom we call God) who created it?

Theists, of course, choose to believe in an eternal God. Others ask where this God came from? They claim, if God can just be there, why can't the Universe just be there?

Is there a difference? Yes, there is, for the universe gives no indication of being eternal. Quite the contrary. It is known to be in a state of gradual decay, with all its primeval energy slowly being dissipated evenly to all its parts –

> Epicurus stated the metaphysical problem centuries ago: "Something obviously exists now, and something never sprang from

nothing." Being, therefore, must have been without beginning. An Eternal Something must be admitted by all, theist, atheist, and agnostic.

But the physical universe could not be this Eternal Something because it is obviously contingent, mutable, subject to decay. How could a decomposing entity explain itself to all eternity? ...

The choice is simple: one chooses either a self existent God or a self existent universe, and the universe is not behaving as if it is self existent. In fact, according to the second law of thermodynamics, the universe is running down like a clock or, better, cooling off like a giant stove. Energy is constantly being diffused or dissipated, that is, progressively distributed throughout the universe. If this process goes on for a few billion more years – and scientists have never observed a restoration of dissipated energy – then the result will be a state of thermal equilibrium, a "heat death", a random degradation of energy throughout the entire cosmos and hence the stagnation of all physical activity.

Naturalists from Lucretius to Sagan have felt that we need not postulate God as long as nature can be considered a self explanatory entity for all eternity. But it is difficult to hold this doctrine if the second law [of thermodynamics] is true and entropy is irreversible. If the cosmos is running down or cooling off, then it could not have been running and cooling forever. It must have had a beginning. (152)

The contrast between an inescapably decaying universe and an immutable God is obvious. It seems much easier to believe in God as the cause of all things than to believe in a mindless universe as the cause of itself.

Someone may still raise the question, "But who caused God?" The question is absurd. It is like asking "Who caused the uncaused?" or "Who made the one who is not made?" God by definition is the Being whose existence, unlike the physical universe, is completely free from any contingency – that is, he is dependent for his existence upon nothing and no one; he is altogether self-sufficient and self-contained.

Yet having said all this, and as sensible as it all may seem, there will always be those who find the arguments unconvincing, or who can raise objections to them. Finally we are left with no choice except to say either that "I do believe" or "I do not believe". For the person who chooses truly to believe, his or her affirmation of faith at once brings its own corroboration. *I believe, therefore I <u>know</u>!*

Nor is a stance of so-called neutrality – the so-called "open mind" – acceptable. For in the matter of the existence or non-existence of God, a refusal to believe is in practice a decision not to believe. And as Pascal showed in his famous *Wager* that is indeed a risky choice!

Many great thinkers have rejected the Christian concept of God, yet have still felt obliged to acknowledge his existence.

---

(152) <u>Evangelical Dictionary of Theology</u>, ed. Walter A. Elwell; Baker Book House, Grand Rapids, Michigan; 1984; art. God, Arguments for the Existence of.

For example Albert Einstein, was often asked whether or not he believed in God. His various replies show that he –

> saw no contradiction between science and religion. As he put it, "The religious inclination lies in the dim consciousness that dwells in humans that all nature, including the humans in it, is in no way an accidental game, but a work of lawfulness, that there is a fundamental cause of all existence." ...
>
> He retained "a profound faith in, and reverence for, the harmony and beauty of what he called the mind of God as it was expressed in the creation of the universe and its laws." He said –
>
> "Try and penetrate with our limited means the secrets of nature and you will find that, behind all the discernible laws and connections, there remains something subtle, intangible and inexplicable. Veneration for this force beyond anything that we can comprehend is my religion. ...
>
> "What separates me from most so-called atheists is a feeling of utter humility toward the unattainable secrets of the harmony of the cosmos." (153)

So I believe in God, and in believing I discover him, and enter into fellowship with him such that he becomes more real than life.

---

(153)   Walter Isaacson, op.cit.

PRAYER AND GOD'S FOREKNOWLEDGE

Like Amos, I might say that I am neither a prophet nor the son of a prophet. Unlike him, I cannot claim any kind of divine infallibility for the ideas I present. Nonetheless I am going to attempt a difficult task. I am going to pretend that I am a philosopher, and under this guise think about the problem of how answered prayer relates to God's foreknowledge.

This is, of course, a problem that arises only in connection with belief in God's total prescience. If the future is at least in some measure open, and therefore as yet unknown to God, then the problem ceases to exist. But if God actually does know *everything* that is going to happen, and if the future is therefore fixed in his knowledge of it, why bother to pray? Prayer would seem a futile exercise.

This problem has troubled many people. Some have even stopped praying, or pray only as a matter of formal routine. The question is: *does God's foreknowledge and immutability make answered prayer impossible?* Does prayer change God, or does it change us? Does it change anything? *Can* it change anything, if the future is already fully known by God?

The question is based on the idea that answered prayer must involve a change in the future that might have been, or in the future God has decreed, or in the future as God presently knows it. But scripture says that God is immutable: *"I am the Lord, I change not!"* If God cannot be changed, if God foreknows the future (which, it is said, must fix the future in the form in which God presently knows it) how can prayer be answered in any real sense of the word? Surely God's foreknowledge and immutability must mean either -

- that prayer is merely a devotional exercise, without any real power to change anything (as it is in Islam); or, if prayer does have power to change things, then
- that God has predetermined the time and content of our prayers so that the answering of them does not cause any disruption either of his program or of his immutable knowledge of the future.

But this would mean that prayer loses either its *voluntary character*, or its *effective power*. It seems impossible that prayer should remain both voluntary and powerful; for if it is both, then the future is continually being changed, depending upon whether or not we choose to pray.

How do those who hold to total prescience solve this logical impasse?

They claim that the argument is true only if God has decreed himself as unwilling to change future events, or to change his purpose, in answer to prayer. But in fact, they say, he has decreed himself as willing to do both, and this decree is part of his immutable character. Here are some examples –

- the repentance of Nineveh changed God's announced intention of destroying the city within forty days (Jo 3:3-10)
- God was quite willing to annihilate Israel, and to begin a new national program through Moses, but Moses stayed the Lord's hand (Ex 32:9-14; Nu 14:11-20; cp also Ps 106:40-46; Je 18:7-10; Jl 2:12-14; Mt 23:37-39.)
- Micah announced the ruin of Jerusalem, but because the people repented, the disaster was averted for a full one hundred years (Je 26:16-19; cp also vs 1-6).
- several other similar examples could be cited.

Then it is said, concerning God's knowledge of the future, that the future God knows is one that includes the answer to our prayers. If we don't pray, the future God knows is a future void of an answer to prayer.

To me, however, we are still left with a dilemma. Whatever God knows of the future (whether in full or in part) he knew yesterday. No action of mine today can be allowed to falsify that knowledge, which seems to lock me inescapably into conforming to that knowledge. But of course, if the future is at least partially open, then there is plenty of room for me to pray and to alter the course of events. And surely that is the very point of the examples cited above? God's announced intentions were changed by prayer!

Perhaps we can arrive at a kind of happy medium; that is, a position where both sides yield some ground and arrive at a reasonable and biblical compromise –

ON CHANGING THE FUTURE

Science fiction writers have grappled with the problem of what might happen if a traveller were able to go back in time and change some significant event in the past (for example, prevent the birth of Napoleon, or cause Nazi Germany to win the battle of Stalingrad). It is generally assumed that for a future observer the past that *was* would at once be changed, and all memory of it would vanish, to be replaced by the memory of the newly created past (for more on this, see number IV below).

This is perhaps a poor illustration of what happens in the mind of God. If he does see the future in total, then that future is the one that emerges from all the choices and decisions we will all finally make. Thus, even if the future seems to us to be in constant flux, his knowledge of it is fixed and unchanging.

In contrast with that, notice that the future belongs to man, not God. God has no future. He dwells in an eternal present. Only what he has created is advancing into the future. The future is part of the human condition, not the divine. We dwell in a time/space continuum, but God dwells in eternity (Is 57:15). Yet it does not follow that God has already created the future nor that he has decreed it in detail. As surely as he created the heavens and the earth and all living things across the span of seven days, why may he not still be unfolding the years of time moment by moment?

The future as such is not decreed by God, (at least not in detail); it is the sum total of human activity. In general it may be said that whatever future God knows is a future determined by our actions, plus the degree of divine involvement invited or demanded by human righteousness or iniquity, and by his own decrees.

We cannot adopt a fatalistic stance and avoid the responsibility of action. We are largely the masters of our own destiny. It lies within the prerogative of the human race to change its own future because, as I see it, the future is at least partly open-ended. It is a mistake to view the future in the same way we view the past. The science fiction writers are wrong – the past is immutable, even to God.

But the *future* is mutable. If man does one day learn to travel through time he will only ever be able to go forward, to hasten the clock, but never to turn it back (even when Hezekiah's sun-dial retreated ten degrees, time itself still continued its relentless advance). The past is fixed and forever unchangeable. Indeed, it apparently has no existence at all, except in our memories and records of it. So there is nothing to go back to.

But the future is not a self-existent entity. It is not pre-created in detail by God. Our future has no existence apart from human activity, intermingled with occasional acts of divine intervention. It will be shaped by God only as much as is necessary to ensure the accomplishment of his universal plan.

Therefore, it seems to me, God has decreed, or fixed the future only in the following ways –

- His kingdom will come and his will done; but the fact that we are commanded to *pray* for this suggests that the time and the manner are flexible in the purpose of God. Also, the coming of *"the last day"* and of the hour of judgment are conditioned by the Lord's desire to bring many sons to glory. His guiding principle must be not to *hasten* the last day, but rather to *delay* it as long as possible, in order to maximise the number of his children. Perhaps the determining factor is not an arbitrarily set date, but rather the point at which there is more risk of the church declining than of continuing to grow.

- God has said from time to time that a certain set of conditions on earth will evoke an inevitable response from heaven. So, *"when the iniquity of the Amorites was full"*, the wrath of God devoured them; or, when the Lord observes faith, he hastens to fulfil his promise to the one believing.

- Biblical prophecy is sufficiently flexible, or sufficiently open in its form, to allow God room to manoeuvre. In both *Old* and *New Testaments* the oracles are seldom, if ever, so plainly stated that all uncertainty is removed. They usually have plenty of space to accommodate slightly (and sometimes even largely) different outcomes. Surely, if the Lord already possesses complete knowledge of all that will ever happen he could have imparted more detail and more specific predictions to the prophets?

- God has so structured the universe that he is able to achieve his full purpose (and will achieve it) without restricting human freedom of choice.
- God is always free to intervene in present human affairs and so to order events that they conform to his will (Is 55:11; Ps 135:6).

TIME TRAVEL

We should be very grateful that time travel, at least into the past is probably impossible, for many authors have shown the extraordinary peril such travel would entail. Alteration of even the smallest past thing or event would have astonishing effects in the present.

In 1992 Douglas Adams published his book *Mostly Harmless*. [154] It begins with an odd but profound paragraph –

> Anything that happens, happens. Anything that in happening causes something else to happen, causes something else to happen. Anything that in happening causes itself to happen again, happens again. It doesn't necessarily do it in chronological order though.

That is a quaint way of expressing the discovery of modern chaos theory, that everything in the universe is intimately connected with everything else. Later in his book, Adams describes it differently. He tells how aeons ago a single neutrino, a tiny particle of matter that is smaller than an atom, plunged out of the sky and struck a single molecule.

---

(154) It was the 5th and final in his series <u>The Hitchhiker's Guide to the Galaxy</u>.

That impact set in motion a chain of events that ended in all clover plants having, not three leaves, but four, with only an occasional three-leaf clover.

This is the paradox faced by all time-travel writers – the smallest interference with the past could have immeasurable consequences in the future.

Ray Bradbury explored this in his 1952 story, *A Sound of Thunder*. A group of people travel back in time sixty million years, and they are warned not to disturb even a blade of grass. Nothing in the past can be changed without placing the future into unknown jeopardy. The tour guide tells the travellers what might happen if their actions inadvertently destroyed, say, a family of mice –

> What about the foxes that'll need those mice to survive? For want of ten mice, a fox dies. For want of ten foxes a lion starves. For want of a lion, all manner of insects, vultures, infinite billions of life forms are thrown into chaos and destruction. Eventually it all boils down to this: fifty-nine million years later, a caveman, one of a dozen on the entire world, goes hunting wild boar or sabre-toothed tiger for food. But you, friend, have stepped on all the tigers in that region. By stepping on one single mouse. So the caveman starves. And the caveman, please note, is not just any expendable man, no! He is an entire future nation. From his loins would have sprung ten sons. From their loins one hundred sons, and thus onward to a civilization. Destroy this one man, and you destroy a race, a people, an entire history of life. It is comparable to slaying some of Adam's grandchildren. The stomp of your foot, on one mouse, could start an earthquake, the effects of which could shake our earth and destinies

down through Time, to their very foundations. With the death of that one caveman, a billion others yet unborn are throttled in the womb. Perhaps Rome never rises on its seven hills. Perhaps Europe is forever a dark forest, and only Asia waxes healthy and teeming. Step on a mouse and you crush the Pyramids. Step on a mouse and you leave your print, like a Grand Canyon, across Eternity. Queen Elizabeth might never be born, Washington might not cross the Delaware, there might never be a United States at all. So be careful. Stay on the Path. Never step off!

One of the travellers did step off the path and killed a butterfly, so that when they got back to their own time the whole world was changed in thousands of different ways. (155)

I am inclined to think that the same kind of problem would bedevil any travel into the future; although of course the problem exists only if the past and the future have some kind of real existence. Even then it would depend upon some means being devised to travel into them. Both propositions are doubtful.

Time, I am happy to say, is not in the hands of science, but in the hand of God, who will ultimately oblige all human activity to fit into his own indestructible and irresistible purpose.

---

(155)   You can read the full story at
        http://www.cs.ru.nl/~freek/books/thunder.sat .

BIBLIOGRAPHY

Addison, Joseph, art. *The Spectator.* December 20th, 1711.

Aquinas, St Thomas(13th century), tr. by Edward Caswall (1848).

Augustine, *The City of God.* tr. by Henry Bettenson; ed. by David Knowles; Penguin Books: London, 1977.

Barclay, William. *Daily Study Bible- New Testament*; The St Andrew Press. 1960.

Bede (A.D. 731) *Ecclesiastical History of the English Nation.*

Berkhof, Louis, *Systematic Theology.* Banner of Truth Trust: Edinburgh, Grand Rapids, USA, 1976.

Bradbury, Ray, *The Hitchhikers Guide to the Galaxy.* Del Ray, 2002

Brison, Bill, *A Short History of Everything.* Doubleday: London, 2003.

Bullett, Gerald. Editor. *Silver Poets of the Sixteenth Century.* J. M. Dent & Sons. London, 1947.

Chant, Barry, *Walking with a Limp.* Openbook Publishers: Adelaide, 2002.

Chant, Ken; *Emmanuel, The Man Who Is God 1 and 2*. Vision Publishing: Australia.

_____. *Strong Reasons.* Vision Publishing: Australia.

_____. *The Cross and the Crown.* Vision Publishing: Australia.

_____. *When the Trumpet Sounds.* Vision Publishing: Australia.

Cicero, Marcus Tullus (106-43 B.C.).*De Divinatione.*

Deventer, Brian van, *"I Believe In ..."* Vision Publishing: Ramona, Ca, 2006.

Donne, John, The Complete English Poems; ed. by A. J. Smith; Penguin Books, 1971.

Elwell, Walter A. Editor. art. G. R. Lewis; *Evangelical Dictionary of Theology.*

Baker Book House: Grand Rapids, Michigan, 1984.

Esdras 2; The Apocrypha

Felleman, Hazel (compiled) *The Best Loved Poems of the American People*. Doubleday: 1936.

Franck, Johann (1649); Poem tr. by Catherine Winkworth (1858).

Gellius, Aulus, *The Attic Nights*. tr. J. C. Rolfe. Loeb Classical Library: 1927.

Gibran, Kahlil. *The Prophet*. Pub. Alfred A. Knopf: New York, 1968.

Herbert, George (1633) *The Elixir*.

Hill, Robert W. Jr. Editor. *Tennyson's Poetry*. W. W. Norton & Co., New York.

International Standard Bible Encyclopedia, in. loc.

James, William. *Principles Of Psychology*.

Johnson, Samuel (1709-1784) The Life of Sir Thomas Browne.

Khayyam, Omar, *The Ruba'iyat*. tr. by Peter Avery and John-Heath-Stubbs. Penguin Classics: 1983.

Kreeft, Peter, *Fundamentals of the Faith*. Ignatius Press: San Francisco, 1988.

Lewis, C. Day, editor. *The Poems of Robert Browning*. The Heritage Press: Norwalk, Connecticut, 1971.

Lloyd, William (1627-1717) Hymn. *Our Times are in Thy Hand*.

Montaigne. Michel de (1533-1592) *Essays of Michel de Montaigne*. tr. by Charles Cotton (1877). Edited by William Carew Hazlitt.

O'Brian, John (a.k.a. Patrick Joseph Hardigan, 1878-1952) Poem *The Birds Will Sing Again*.

Oxford Companion to English Literature, The. art. *Dramatis Personae*. Oxford University Press. 1985

Patrides, C. A. *Introduction to Thomas Browne - The Major Works*.

Pearlman, Myer, *Knowing the Doctrines of the Bible*. Gospel Publishing House: Springfield, 1937.

Plass, Edward M. *What Luther Says*. Concordia Pub. House: Saint Louis, Mo., 1959.

Sterne, Laurence (1759) *Tristram Shandy*. Oxford University Press: Oxford, 1983 edition.

Tatian (120- 185) *Address to the Greeks*.

Watts, Isaac, *The Psalms of David*. 1719.

Wesley, Samuel Jr. *Poems on Several Occasions*. (1736)

Wesley, John, *Wesley's Sermons*. 1872 edition.

Westminster Confession of Faith (1646)

BIBLE COMMENTARIES

Anders, Max, editor. *Holman New Testament Commentary*. B & H Publishing Group: Nashville, Tennessee, 2004.

Barnes, Albert (1798-1870) *Notes on the Bible*.

Bible Background Commentary. Intervarsity Press: Nottingham, U.K., 1993.

Calvin, John (1509-1564) *Calvin's Commentaries*.

Clarke, Adam (1715-1832) *Commentary on the Bible*.

NIV Commentary, The. College Press: Joplin, Missouri, 1996.

Excell, Joseph S. and Spence-Jones, H. D. M., editors. *The Pulpit Commentary*. 1881.

Gaebelein, Frank E. Editor. *The Expositor's Bible Commentary*. Zondervan Publishers: Grand Rapids, Michigan.

Gill, John (1690-1771) *Exposition of the Entire Bible*.

Hawker, Robert, *The Poor Man's Commentary On The Whole Bible*. 1850.

Henry, Matthew, *Commentary On The Whole Bible*. Marshall, Morgan, and Scott: London, 1953

Hodge, Charles, (1797-1878).*A Commentary on Ephesians*. Intervarsity Press.

Interpreter's Bible, The. Abingdon Press: New York, 1952.

Ironside, H. A. *Expository Commentary* (1876-1951).

IVP New Testament Commentary Series, The. Intervarsity Press:

Nottingham, UK.

Jamieson, R, A. Fausett and D. Brown, *A Commentary on the Old and New Testaments*, 1871.

Johnson B. W. *The People's New Testament*. 1891.

_____. *The People's New Testament Commentary*. Word Search Corporation: Nashville, Tennessee, 2010.

Macdonald, William, *Believer's Bible Commentary*. Thomas Nelson Publishers: 1989.

Nelson's New Illustrated Bible Commentary. Thomas Nelson Inc., New York, 1999.

New Testament Commentary, The. Baker's Publishing House: Grand Rapids, Michigan, 1987.

Poole, Matthew, *Matthew Poole's Commentary*. 1685

Preacher's Commentary, The. Word Inc., Nashville, Tennessee, 1992.

Preacher's Outline and Sermon Bible. Word Search Corporation: Nashville, Tennessee, 2010.

Robertson A. T. *Word Pictures in the New Testament*. 1933.

Stern, David H. *Jewish New Testament Commentary*. Jewish New Testament Publications Inc., Clarksville, Maryland; 1982.

Trapp, John, *Commentary On The Old And New Testaments* (1601-1669).

Vincent, Marvin R. *Vincent's Word Studies*. 1886

Walvoord, John and Zuck, Roy, *The Bible Knowledge Commentary*. Cook Communications: Colorado Springs, Colorado, 1989.

Wesley, John, *Explanatory Notes on the Whole Bible* (1703-1791).

Wiersbe, Warren W. *Wiersbe's Expository Outlines*. Pub. David C. Cook: Colorado Springs, Colorado

Wiseman, D. J. General editor. *Tyndale Old Testament Commentaries*. Intervarsity Press.

BIBLE VERSIONS

In addition to the *KJV* or *Authorised Version* of the Bible, the following versions or translations are cited, or were consulted by the author of this work.

CEV – *Contemporary English Version*; the American Bible Society, New York, NY; 1995.

ESV – *English Standard Version*; Crossway Bibles, a publishing ministry of Good News Publishers; Wheaton, Illinois; 2001.

GNB – *Good News Bible*; Second Edition, by the American Bible Society; New York, NY; 1992.

GW –*God's* Word; God's Word to the Nations Bible Society; Cleveland, Ohio; 1995.

JPS – *The JPS* Bible; the Jewish Publication Society; Philadelphia, PA; 1995.

ISV – *International Standard Version*, v. 1.2.2; The ISV Foundation, La Mirada, CA; 2001.

NET – *The Net Bible*; Biblical Studies Press; Richardson, Texas; 2006.

NIV – *New International Version*; Zondervan Bible Publishers, Grand Rapids, Michigan; 1978.

NJB – *New Jerusalem Bible*; Doubleday & Co. Inc; Garden City, New York; 1985

NRSV – *New Revised Standard Version*; the Division of Christian Education of the National Council of the Churches of Christ in the USA; 1989.

REB – *Revised English Bible with Apocrypha*; Oxford University Press; 1989.

YLT – *Young's Literal Translation*; by NJ Young; 1898.

www.ingramcontent.com/pod-product-compliance
Lightning Source LLC
Chambersburg PA
CBHW070533170426
43200CB00011B/2407